A Corner of Paradise

Paradise

A love story (with the usual reservations)

VINTAGE BOOKS
London

Published by Vintage 2014

2 4 6 8 10 9 7 5 3 1

Copyright © Brian Thompson 2013

Brian Thompson has asserted his right under the Copyright, Designs
and Patents Act 1988 to be identified as the author of this work

First published in Great Britain in 2013 by
Chatto & Windus

Vintage
Random House, 20 Vauxhall Bridge Road,
London SW1V 2SA

www.vintage-books.co.uk

Addresses for companies within The Random House Group Limited
can be found at: www.randomhouse.co.uk/offices.htm

The Random House Group Limited Reg. No. 954009

A CIP catalogue record for this book
is available from the British Library

ISBN 9780099581864

The Random House Group Limited supports the Forest Stewardship
Council® (FSC®), the leading international forest-certification
organisation. Our books carrying the FSC label are printed on FSC®-
certified paper. FSC is the only forest-certification scheme supported
by the leading environmental organisations, including Greenpeace.
Our paper procurement policy can be found at:
www.randomhouse.co.uk/environment

Printed and bound by Clays Ltd, St Ives Plc

For Wendy Hill

'We only have our story, and it isn't ours.'

José Ortega y Gasset

CONTENTS

1 The Cottage   1

2 A Gift of Dreams   4

3 In The Beginning   13

4 A Piano In This Wood By Chance   24

5 Lady of the Lavender Mist   31

6 Telling Us Apart   38

7 House Warming   54

8 Paper Games and Moonlight   71

9 Some Deaths   84

10 Inconsolable   99

11 Picnics and Flea Markets   116

12 The Green Tunnel   131

13 La Frairie   145

14 The Year of the Mobilette   158

15 The Dinner Gong   173

16 Keeping Mum   189

17 The End Game   204

18 Finally . . .   211

    The Eulogy   213

The Cottage

Since you died, I have felt the world falling down, sometimes with nothing more than the sensation of dust running through my fingers, sometimes like the side of the house collapsing. Though I have watchful and caring children I have no one to talk to about these uneasy shocks and tremors – the only person that would understand the pickle I'm in is, of course, you. And there's the pain of it. You were loved and admired: you have gone. It's because I don't know where you have gone that I persist in talking to you. I try to talk to you every night. I read until my eyes ache, switch out the light, and drift into sleep telling you what's been happening. It is not always news you want to hear.

What I would really like to create for your memorial is an empty cottage somewhere to which I could send you daily cards and letters. It would be remote, to suit your habit of solitude, but not so bleak that plants did not grow there. Each spring I would of course forward your seed catalogues and order up shrubs and perennials from your favourite nurseries. It would be a matter of wonder to the postman that while there was never a sign of you, the garden flourished. On the other side of the letter box, the envelopes and cards would cascade gently towards the kitchen.

There is a catch, of course: you left (as we all will do) without a forwarding address. Last night I was drinking in the garden of an Oxford pub called the Marsh Harrier in the magic hour of low sun and blue shadows. One end of the garden is bounded by a huge and dense weeping willow, maybe thirty feet tall. Almost absentmindedly, while talking to my grandson about road-race cycling and the like, I donated it to your landscape, in memory of your love of trees. Nevertheless, this place, which is as real to me as my own existence, stubbornly refuses to give up its location. Maybe the views from the windows look out onto a milky eternity; or maybe only a distant power station, surrounded by cow pastures and caravan sites.

It is a game I play with myself, to keep at bay a near total desolation. All my life I have rowed, as must we all, with my back to the future. And now, at last, I have arrived. You once said to a woman friend, 'I hope I don't go first, because without me he couldn't find his way to the front door.' There is an even more terrible truth in this than you realised.

This is the story of our time together, which lasted almost exactly half my life. It began with two more or less amicable divorces in 1973, leaving the two of us together in a crabby terrace house in Yorkshire and a small cloud of children, some more forgiving than others. I have thought for a long time about how to tell what happened next, without upsetting the sensibilities of these children, all of them older now than we were at the time. They must make of what follows what they will, for this is not their story, but ours. And, very much to your taste, I think, I begin with piece of misdirection that leads all the same to something very important to us both later on.

A Gift of Dreams

In 1935 Gaston Dujardin saw his first aeroplane. Announced by its belching engine note, it flew directly over his house and courtyard, a transit taking no more than a few seconds. He ran out into the road and watched as it made a slow banking turn over Madame Edith's fields of stubble, the pilot perfectly visible in his open cockpit, the banana yellow of the wings and fuselage set off by the green of the oaks that lay along the road to La Fontaine. Then the plane levelled and wobbled away, leaving Gaston with his jaw hanging open.

That night, he discussed what he had seen and what he planned to do about it with his neighbour.

'You don't think you ought to clean the place up first, Gaston? Let's be frank about it, shovel some of the manure, wash down the cows? Everybody wishes you well, you know that.'

The dog seemed to know what was being said. He slunk away into the dark of the second room, head low. His neighbour, Gerard, was reminded of the way some wives behaved when men sat down to argue. The dog was saying, he's a shame, a disgrace, but what can I do? I'm just his beast.

'I am going to build such a plane,' Gaston repeated. 'I shall fly around and wave to you. Not too high, mind you. Maybe not if it's raining. Or windy.'

'But a plane, my old friend! Not an easy task.'

'I have a picture of it in my head.'

They said of Gaston in the village that with just another spoonful of blood from his father's side he could have turned out dangerous: instead he was as steady and gentle as one of his cows. Children who mocked him had their ears cuffed by their parents. His barns were falling down, his chickens roamed the street, he himself was announced by the stink of his clothes and skin. He cut his hair with the clasp knife that every farmer carried, pulled his own teeth. He was what the French call, in an affectionate but cautionary word for it, *un originale*.

'Well,' Gerard conceded with a diplomatic shrug. 'It's something to do in the winter. You don't think you need a plan at all?'

'I told you, I have a plan,' Gaston said gently.

He was a small Charentais farmer, impoverished, famously sardonic, and incurious about anything that lay outside the more or less shapeless hamlet of Breuil. There he had friends who egged him on, all of them men. They gathered to drink and be preposterous for a few snatched hours before the drudgery of fieldwork claimed them the next morning. The memorable years for Gaston were those that had to do with the weather – autumn gales from the north-east that ripped off tiles and brought down ancient trees, or unseasonable spring droughts that ruined the vines. On wet days he stood under the barns and amused himself by inscribing with a rusty nail flower patterns in the soft stone of a pillar; or scribbling an imaginary income with a pencil or a bit of charcoal. From time to time his rich nephews would pitch up on their way to see his sister, who lived a little way up the hill.

Half a kilometre away the woods began, where during the war the boys had gathered to plot against the Germans and which also contained the forgotten remains of a tenth-century motte-and-bailey castle. The most recent structure was an open-sided shack for the *chasseurs*, who gathered to drink and smoke and compare their bags. And, no doubt, to gossip about women and the secrets of the marriage bed. Gaston had neither a gun nor a woman. He had never left the hamlet in which he was born, had no car, and was superficially uncultured. His only reading material was the newspaper in which his fish was wrapped at the Tuesday market in Beauvais-sur-Matha. Once or twice a year he lurched along to burial services at the cemetery, half an hour's walk away. He was, despite his boisterous good humour, as good as dead and buried himself.

For eight years following, he collected the materials for his plane – scraps of sheet tin, lengths of timber, ruined gauges from the auto wreckers' yard at St Hilaire, bales of wire. The first thing he fabricated was the easiest – a bicycle wheel to which eight staves were attached: eight because that was how he remembered the look of the propeller in flight. The wingspan of the plane was dictated by the width of the barn in which it was housed. Since he was never going to find enough tin to finish the job, he began to form and shape the rest with woven straw and cow dung. He found that, once dry, the dung took an incredible high polish, subtly brown and arrestingly glassy. But, as everyone in the village warned him, a plane was no small thing.

His was the last house in the hamlet. A couple of hundred metres away, the communal boundary was marked by a short red and white pillar set in the verge of the road. To walk past it was to enter foreign parts. Breuil itself lay in a shallow valley and was part of the commune of Bresdon. Gaston's place was hardly a warm welcome to strangers from the south. Three immense barns and a high wall hid the house, which was sideways on to the road. Only the most curious of night travellers could interpret the crashing and banging of Gaston and his cronies for what it was – Charentais hospitality and the power of (generally) very young brandy.

Two such travellers did in fact come into the yard one night. They were forced-labourers on the run from Bordeaux. Gaston accommodated them in the turnip cellar, not crouched in a corner but buried alive until the morning patrol of Germans passed, three plump and amiable men on bicycles, their rifles slung across their backs. Arriving by horseback would have suited these examples of the master race better, a Kübelwagen even more so. But everyone knew that their overriding business was not to be drafted to the Russian Front. Like Gaston himself, they were looking for the quiet life.

It was this house that Elizabeth North and I bought in the early 1990s. We had lived together for twenty years and were hardly adventurers: in appearance we looked, well, comfy. The kind of people we resembled – and the ferry had been stuffed with them – lived further south in the Dordogne, where an English-language newspaper reported the local cricket scores. Its feature pages were, on the whole, jolly accounts of local tradesmen, recipes that were worth the cooking, village gossip and the cheapest way to tile a swimming pool.

The impulse to buy a house in France was nearly all mine. I cannot say it was entirely rational, and first impressions confirmed this. Most of Gaston's plane had disappeared but he had recycled some of the materials to make a form of central heating, which was to reroute the carbon monoxide from the chimney and dispel it in smoky gusts through the main room. Rotting windows and a missing pane or two created enough drafts to keep him safe. The only source of water was a standpipe in the cow byres, and to evacuate his bowels he nudged the cows away with his elbows and squatted. He cooked on an open fire and, when he had eaten, gave the plate to his dog to lick clean before putting it away in a cupboard. Mice ate his curtains.

In the last phase of his life he took on an electricity supply and amused himself by screwing scavenged porcelain light switches to various walls, none of which were wired to the mains. The chestnut floors had fallen in. The *grenier*, where he had once kept his chickens (and his rats) could only be reached by an ancient and worm-eaten ladder. Little by little his life dwindled away, lit by a single forty-watt bulb. His well, which was eighteen metres deep, was a raggedy hole in the ground from which the windlass had disappeared. In the yard, what wasn't limestone was concrete. There was not a blade of grass anywhere to be seen.

It says a great deal about our relationship that Liz tolerated my enthusiasm for this nightmare property.

Strictly speaking we were on holiday, with only half an idea of buying property. We had been shown around by a local estate agent, accompanied by his sidekick, a middle-aged English woman who explained that there were two types of wine, red and white; that the correct form of address to the natives of this country was *Bon Jour!*; and so on. This poor woman had never met anyone quite like Liz and was astonished when we said goodbye at a property she recommended as being typically French. It was owned by a stringy old gay and his young friend, who stalked about in Speedos and sunglasses. Whatever they promised each other when they got together, it was not domestic bliss. The place was filthy. In the bathroom a plate of herring bones sat on the toilet seat.

'*Traitez comme chez vous,*' the vendor encouraged from the doorway. He too was naked save for some Hawaiian shorts.

'What did he say?' Liz demanded icily.

'Oh, he's apologising for the mess, I expect.'

Liz turned on the old man and raked him with a single glance. '*Moi, je me trouve toute cette galère épouvantable, m'sieu.*' And left.

We found Gaston's place next day almost by accident and under our own steam. To review the situation, we stayed in the Hôtel du Commerce at Beauvais-sur-Matha, bought by the commune as a touristical venture. Most nights we dined alone.

'All right. About Gaston's place. Would you say you were good at do-it-yourself?' she asked amiably enough.

'Not in the fullest sense, no.'

'Are you a practical person? In any sense of the word at all?'

'I have put up bookshelves,' I said, a touch too stiffly.

'You haven't signed anything, though, have you?'

'Not yet. But think about it, Liz. I'm giving you my reckless side here, my daredevil energy.'

'Mmm,' she said. 'Your notorious recklessness.'

'And daredevil energy.'

'Or foolhardiness.'

The bar in this place closed at ten and we lay in bed, smoking and drinking supermarket white wine.

'The situation is tense,' I suggested.

Gaston's farmhouse lay four kilometres away, surrounded by huge fields of maize. There were no enchanting features to the landscape, which was generally as flat as a billiard table. Well within the memory of the commune, wheat from these fields had been cut by hand and carried away by ox-cart. In those days everybody made their own brandy and grew their own vegetables. Women wore black, men cinched their trousers with rope, the better class with braces. Even the smallest of children could manage a herd of cows or trap birds inside little wicker baskets.

Gaston's war was their war. They were an occupied country but the local overlords were perspiring men in grey who patrolled the empty lanes on bicycles. Certainly there was a garrison at Neuvicq-le-Château but who had ever had business there in the days of peace? As for Paris, it was an impossibly remote city, of little practical consequence. What governed were the seasons and the inescapable drudgery of fieldwork. No bomber streams flew overhead; there were no flak guns. Even when the Germans left and the Americans arrived from the south, life continued much as it had for generations. Communities like this contributed next to nothing to the political history of France. The two great festivals that survived were the *Quatorze*, when the mayor donated an alfresco meal, which it was social suicide to ignore, and the *frairie*, a harvest-time get-together and gossip mill.

'If you buy the place, I shall look out for other GB plates and tell them of your presence,' the vendor of Gaston's little corner of this paradise promised.

'No, you must send them on their way. Tell them the place is cursed with leprosy.'

This man, who was one of Gerard's children and a rich fund of Gaston stories, pushed out his lower lip for a moment and then shrugged. 'I can do that,' he said. 'Have you come to live here for good?'

'No. But every summer, say from May to September.'

He smiled, as though it was the first piece of common sense he had heard me utter.

'You have retired?'

'Madame Elizabeth and I are both writers.'

'You have come to write about us?'

'Absolutely not.'

'You are a rich Englishman looking for a *maison secondaire*,' he suggested.

'Just that. Though we are not rich.'

Liz sat in the shade of the house listening to all this, a wet chiffon scarf over her head, a bottle of Evian in her fist, examining her mosquito bites. Her face had the faint air of abstraction she had carried about with her since she was a child. The first of dozens of spiral-bound notebooks she bought in France lay on the ground beside her.

'We are not rich,' she confirmed.

Even a little further investigation could have shown us there were better places to buy, in towns with amenities like shops and cafés, dispensaries and hospitals. In such places there might be a castle, even. Left to herself, I know she would have chosen central heating, train connections to Paris, daily vegetable markets, a good bookshop. In the Hôtel du Commerce she lay on her stomach reading *Great Crimes of Passion in the Poitou Region*. The one that interested her most, about which she had begun to make notes, was the story of a farmer who had kept his servant chained in a barn for twelve years. She was perhaps thinking of Gaston and the story of his plane, his charmingly named cow, Leonie, the whimsical touches he had left scattered about, his eccentric bachelordom.

'It doesn't do for a man to live alone,' she muttered, just before we fell asleep.

'That will never happen to us.'

'To me, you mean. I hope not.'

3

In The Beginning

Our life together dated from the autumn of 1973 and was the consequence of two divorces. Both our former partners (who were unknown to each other) were done with Yorkshire and went off to other parts with other people, never to return. We stayed put. We were not the purposive and thrusting members of these first marriages, but more like the fallen masts and rigging that needed to be cut away before the ship could rejoin the fleet. Images like this did not occur to me at the time. Nonetheless, whatever was lacking in us had found us out. Put baldly, the divorces would have taken place in any case with or without our contribution.

For the previous nine years, I had worked for a small educational charity, founded in 1909 by a meeting in the Rowntree Cocoa Works, York. Its original purpose had been to offer basic education in child-rearing and house-hold management to the poor of Leeds. By the time of my tenure as Warden things had changed in tune with the times. We taught painting and print-making, pottery and sculpture; French, German, Italian and Russian – all strongly reinforced by a range of WEA classes that (I hoped) would encourage the intellectual cadres that actually ran the city – school governors, local councillors and the like. It was ramshackle and uproarious, careless and on occasions politically wilful enough to trouble the local authority, on whose grant we depended. We made films, we performed plays.

There was much about the place to be proud of, and quite a lot to deprecate. One of the things about growing old is that I dream about this job, always waking with profound relief that I have not burned the premises down, nor seen the arrest of some of the more volatile tutors on grounds of public indecency. For example, the American painter Frank Howard once mounted an exhibition of exquisite line drawings entitled 'Twelve Architectural Suggestions' that I considered of impeccable purity. They were in fact renderings of his wife's tenderest and most intimate parts.

'I feel sorry for you,' my soon to be ex-wife said. 'You're going to be one of those men who hangs around the BBC bar with nothing but old jokes and green room stories. Who's going to take you on?'

'Well, there may be someone.'

When I mentioned who that might be, she brightened.

'If you can get her, that would be excellent. Give her a ring, ask her what she thinks. She could be your only hope.'

She was right. Although my private life was just short of chaotic, in career terms I was well placed. I had only to act a little more wisely to head towards the fool's gold of a pension and measured retirement. It was a long way off but the signposts could be relied upon and the path was hardly steep. There was a catch. That summer

I had resigned in order to write for a living. It was the equivalent of picking up the loaded revolver and doing the decent thing, as was suggested by the Leeds Education Department none too subtly. Mists at once rolled in, obscuring a landscape I was never to see again. I made the call.

'I don't see why not,' Liz said about the proposal that we should live together. Her telephone manner was crisp, I thought. And all the better for that.

'I'm not much good on the telephone,' she said, softening.

There were a few seconds of silence and then, artful minx, she replaced the receiver.

I brought to the new relationship a great deal of unfinished business with my parents and a portmanteau of other guilty feelings – about a failed marriage, the abandonment of a career in adult education, the future of my three children and the curse of a disruptive personality inherited from my grandfather, that cocky Lambeth chancer. Much more to the point, at the time that we got together, I was broke. The lustrous radio producer Susannah Simon took pity on me and my first commission as a full-time writer came from serving up overheated short stories for a Capital Radio series called *Moment of Terror*. It went out just before midnight and was heard by drunks, insomniacs, and (I imagined) madmen skinning up in urban squats.

Liz would have come to live with me had I been an insurance clerk, a school caretaker, or almost anything else. I would have pursued her to the ends of the earth had she been a dinner lady – or a tango instructor. However, we were asking a lot of each other, besotted as we were. From the very beginning we ruled out getting married, at first to protect the feelings of the youngest of her children, but later on because it seemed irrelevant; later still, redundant. This decision had one particular consequence, which, had we been different people, we might have foreseen. Try as I might, I began and continued as the disruptive and untrustworthy interloper, the stranger from a different part of the forest, without the necessary tribal markings and speaking gibberish. What was in play was not so much antagonism, nor even dislike. Quite simply, I was from the wrong tribe. My mother thought the same way about it.

'This woman, who you say is older than you, does she have kiddies?'

'Four.'

'She has four kiddies, her father was an admiral in the navy and they come from Dorset. Well, Brizie, I would say, in all seriousness, you need your bloody head examining.'

We had met at a writing class of which I was the tutor and she the enigmatic student – poised, very alert, cautious in turn – and far too gifted to waste her time on what I might have to say. I refunded her fee and told her to go away and write a novel. It was published the following year and I read my copy while attending an educational conference at New College, Oxford. I was swiped sideways by the wit and elegance of the writing. Wandering moon-struck across Christ Church meadows would have been the poetic gesture, had I any poetry in me. Instead, I sat in the King's Arms drinking pints and flipping beermats. Something wonderful has happened, I said to myself over and over again. I felt like the garage mechanic who slouches out to service a customer in some out-of-the-way petrol station and is confronted by a red Ferrari with foreign plates.

'I wish you *were* a mechanic,' she said dolefully when I told her of this simile. We were leaning against the bonnet of her much-dinted, wilfully recalcitrant Renault 4, just back from its annual holiday excursion to Cornwall, a journey she described as akin to driving into a sock. On the backseat were discarded sweaters and anoraks, socks and sandals, a short history of a woman with four children. At my suggestion we met in a supermarket car park out along the ring road.

'This is ridiculous,' I heard myself saying, taking her hand. It was dusk and the air was filled with the chatter of trolley wheels and final warnings from exasperated mothers to their fretful children.

'They say the vegetables here are very good.'

'The title of your next book, maybe.'

'My next book,' she chided gently, glancing at her watch. 'I have to get back. Shouldn't we kiss or something?'

That is how it began. A year later we were an item. And about that, there is this to say: neither of us was the finished article, perhaps never would be. We had no plans, no strategies. I had published one novel as that very obvious thing, a graduate with a salary, afraid to let go of the river bank and yet wanting to stay in the boat. Liz had published one novel – a far better one – stuck in that same boat but staring incredulously at the tussock of grass that had once been her anchor, the woman who she was expected to be – so badly described by a social class of which I knew nothing. In my eyes, an admiral's daughter was no small thing.

'What do you most want?' she asked in those early heady days.

'To earn the respect of people whom I respect.'

'Updike, for example.'

'Nearer to home. Much nearer to home. Tell me what you most want.'

'To be taken seriously.' She thought for a moment. 'To have the chance of taking myself seriously.'

'I am your man,' I said, with far too much fervour.

There was, nevertheless, much I did not know about this new family, as, for example, the utter sacredness of certain place names: Havant, Dorset, Tresawle, Gibraltar. It was a matter of wonder to Liz's children that I had never read *Winnie the Pooh* nor *The Wind in the Willows*, never played mah-jong, knew nothing about Divine Light, Black Sabbath or magic mushrooms. I had never eaten pizza or tuna, smoked dope or ridden a horse. Of the four standing stones that indicated the lost grandeur of this family's history, I had never visited any of them.

We started out together in a tiny terrace house in Harrogate, which the previous owners had done their best to gentrify. It was a losing battle in the kind of back street where gloomy men grew tomatoes in pots and knickers put out to dry in the yard were stolen by some mysterious night-stalker, who, when he was caught, turned out to have a museum of the same. We came to this house with three teenage girls, a monosyllabic boy, a cat, dog, horse and two cages of rabbits. These were no small amendments to what the neighbours considered a proper way of going on.

Almost at once, the crabby little rooms began to fill with books and records, mismatched crockery, ancient and

18

moth-eaten carpets, all the signs of a cheerfully disordered life. White wine bottles marched briskly through the house, swinging along to Count Basie. After midnight, my new life-partner's habit was to sprawl in the bath, smoking and reading. It was the most private room in the house, for we had found out that pillow talk was monitored by the girls, who listened at the grate in their bedroom, immediately above ours.

'The trouble with you,' I whispered, after only a fortnight of living together, 'is that you think you're smarter than me.'

'Oh dear,' Liz murmured, looking for somewhere to stub her Gauloise. 'Perhaps I should have made that clear right from the outset.'

'Your children resent me to hell.'

'Who cares what anybody else thinks?' she cried. 'I love you – and for what it's worth, I am warmer here than in any house I've ever lived in.'

This was a piece of realism of the kind I soon got used to. There was nothing lovey-dovey about us. Over time, there was hardly a detail of each other's history we did not discover, while agreeing that however glorious whatever it was that brought us together, it did not do to ask too many questions of it. How love worked, what it meant, remained an unbroachable mystery. At the very least, being in love meant learning where one person leaves off and the other begins. Living together was an exercise in asymmetry.

I was foolish enough to think that I could charm her children into liking me, or at least tolerating me – that old story. One of the innovations I proposed was that we should all eat the same evening meal together at the same table. It was an unwelcome novelty. The food was no more meagre than the children had eaten before: Liz had been held to a ridiculously small household budget by her former husband, from which she first deducted the cost of cigarettes and chocolate. We were poor now in a way neither of us had practice in. Among the children (with the exception of Thomas) there was a chic in playing at paupers that had nothing to do with their actual social background. They were slumming: it was the fashion. In the beginning at least, the house resembled a night hostel, run by an eternally patient cook and a bad-tempered caretaker.

'Who is that surly round-shouldered boy that just sloped in?' a visitor from London asked one rainy midnight.

'My daughter,' Liz replied.

He nodded, kneading a squash ball in the palm of his hand and nudging the dog away with his knee. Earlier in the week, what Liz described as a slug the size of a milk bottle had come through the floorboards. In the previous week to that, I was redecorating when I discovered that the plaster over the fireplace was only prevented from falling into the room by a faded sheet of Edwardian wallpaper, on which age and damp had imprinted what looked like a map of Indonesia. I painted it over hastily, not without guilty testing of the chimney breast. Under my hand what seemed like broken digestive biscuits grated against each other.

The second house we bought in Harrogate was bigger and a little more sophisticated. It was considered by estate agents a good address and the neighbours were interesting. The faintly owlish Thomas went from there to preparatory boarding school – very much against his mother's wishes but as a placatory gesture to her ex-husband, who had put him down for Stowe. Her second daughter Sophie was married from this house, not just to any old body but the son of a rich solicitor.

It was here also that we began the habit of New Year's Eve parties, founded on the precept that it was better to have far too many guests than too few. We acquired a small reputation for goofing-off.

'You know so many utterly ghastly people,' Liz's aunt from Florida complained. 'I was talking yesterday to a neighbour of yours, a boy who paints Spitfires flying from what he calls the rosy-cheeked buttocks of nuns.'

'Not an entirely serious person, would you say?'

'I think not,' Sheila drawled. 'I don't at all mind people being unintelligent, but there has to be style at the back of it somewhere. Be careful you don't lose your way, my poor darlings.'

This from a woman who bound her lower jaw to her upper with a chiffon scarf before sleep every night; someone for whom the last cup of breakfast coffee was followed by the first Bloody Mary of the day. In Florida she did a weekly stint on the radio, playing what she called the fizzy little third movements of symphonic works and inter- viewing crazy old film stars who hardly knew where they were any longer, nor cared, so long as there was a micro- phone in the room. Her show was enormously popular.

'I think I know as much about nuns' buttocks as that insufferable little squit,' she muttered absent-mindedly. 'Who is the child I hear picking out chords on the piano?'

'My youngest son,' I supplied. 'He wants to be a jazz musician.'

'How dull.'

'You think so?'

'I'm sure he is an adorable little chap but I was dearest chums with Tommy Beecham, my darling. That does make a difference, don't you think?'

Sheila was part of the smoke-and-mirrors family background that Liz had been born to. She had a good war, buzzing about London being glamorous and irresistible to American staff officers. Though she worked for the BBC, she never walked round the corner to Fitzrovia. Her preferred watering holes were Claridge's and the Ritz. There was another aunt who had met and spoken with Christ in the Berlin Tiergarten shortly after the Great War. He directed her to go to Bangalore and help found the Church of South India, which, to everybody's astonishment, she did. Eilean, Liz's mother, was the relict of Admiral Sir Dudley North, brutally and shamefully dismissed by Winston Churchill in 1940. In his day, Dudley had commanded the royal yacht and Eilean had a small treasury of stories about the Prince of Wales at his ease. Somewhere or other in the house, stuffed in a back drawer, was a silver cigarette box signed by David for courtly services rendered.

'I have a little grandson, Lady North,' Mrs Wiggins, the cleaner, confided, 'and every Sat'day he goes into town for his sweeties. And then he rings me up and says "Hello, Granny, I love you".'

'How terribly, terribly tiresome,' Eilean said, mumbling on a biscuit. 'Can't you stop him doing that?'

It would have been dizzying, all this, had Liz herself set any store by it. She did not. Endlessly good-tempered, with exquisite manners, there was at the very heart of her a contradictory impulse. She was twice as glamorous as Sheila, on the way to being as spiritual as anybody who ever joined the Church of South India and a better anecdotalist than her mother (though with the same phenomenal memory for the names of people's dogs). But there was a problem. What set her apart (after the first fine careless raptures) was the undisclosed part of her nature. She was by temperament and inclination a solitary. It shows in all the photographs taken of her. What seems like insecurity is actually a balance of caution. She does not want to be captured by a photograph.

4

A Piano In This Wood
By Chance

We first met the Tofts and the Lowdens at a party in Stan
Barstow's house. Mike Toft and Olga, Ken Lowden and
Monica, were couples who had, seemingly, lived next door
to each other forever, starting out in crabby flats and
presently located in a housing tract in North Leeds once
beyond their wildest dreams. Michael had been a trainee
coalface worker for a fortnight or so, before choosing
more congenial work above ground as a cinema projectionist, later on a wallpaper salesman. Olga worked in a
cigarette kiosk. Ken was a lab technician at Leeds Poly.
Monica worked in a shoe shop. They were collectively
four of the truest friends to be had anywhere.

They lived in a long road of identical houses, kept up
to showroom standards with beautifully mown grass
aprons in the front and gleaming cars in the short drive-
ways. After they had been there ten years, someone had
the bright idea of throwing an anniversary party. All the
women and children gathered in one house and all the men

in another. (This seemed to everyone invited a thoroughly unexceptional arrangement.) After the husbands and fathers had given the six-packs of Tetley's a hammering, Michael broached the question: 'So what 'ave we learned in these last ten years?'

There were a variety of answers. Not all of them were to the point. Gary and his wife had got hold of tickets to the Royal Enclosure at Ascot one year. True, he had forgotten to take his top hat off when bowing to the Queen Mother, but he was thirty yards away and felt he had got away with it. Frank, meanwhile, had followed Leeds United to every away game since the year dot. His wife did all the mortgage stuff and she was happy enough. So what was there to say? Mel's girl had done well at Allerton Grange High School, parlayed that into a university course in theology at Reading and was now in London, unhappy as hell.

'Doing what, like?'

'Selfridge's.'

The man who had convened the meeting cleared his throat.

'To answer Michael's question direct, when we moved in we used to ask ourselves "What will happen if we are made redundant?" Ten years on, we're asking "What will happen when we're made redundant?"'

'It put the wind up me, I can tell you,' Michael confessed to me. 'What's more, it's one of those poxy no-smoking houses. We 'ad to stand in the cowing garden for a fag. Just like a bunch of bloody dustmen.'

To like Ken and Michael, you had also to like Tetley's bitter and their nightly rendezvous at a pub called the Dexter, which was part of the estate and built (I always imagined) to stop local residents attacking each other with hatchets and electric bread knives. They always drank four pints before stumping home – never five and never three and a cheeky half. At turning-out time, they would walk a couple of hundred yards to their neighbouring front doors and say goodnight with an economical grunt.

I envied them. On the occasions that the womenfolk went down the Dexter with us, we would all end up back at Michael's house listening to his Stan Kenton record (he had only the one) and – to signal Liz's presence – a glass or two of Scotch and a bit of Battenberg cake. Monica acted as Mike's literary adviser.

'I got such an interesting biography of Sinclair Lewis out of the library today, Michael.'

'Aye, Red Lewis they called him. Well, make a few notes, Mon, and let me have them. But the bloke that fascinates me more is that Traven fella, him that wrote *Treasure of the Sierra Madre*. You'll know his work, Liz.'

'She hasn't got time for the books you like, Michael,' Olga objected.

'Eh, she's read practically everything that's ever been printed, Olga my love. I don't know how she does it.'

But Olga, who was tiny but also feisty, had an answer for that.

'Well, for a start she don't have to go round selling loads of wallpaper to corner shops that don't want it,' she snapped.

I proposed Monica for a vacant seat on the BBC Regional Council and there her common sense and compassion flourished. She was, as the Head of Broadcasting put it, with collar-tugging gratitude, 'real'. Liz found my enthusiasm for the Gang of Four baffling, but was seduced by Michael's artless honesty.

'I have had a rotten bloody life, Elizabeth, but at least my father weren't some poxy admiral. It's left its mark on you, all that la-di-dah stuff. And as far as I can make out, that whole family never had a pot to piss in.'

'You've had a rotten life, have you?' Olga called from her spotless kitchen.

'Just a way of talking, Olga my love. But you, Liz. How you ever ended up with our kid here baffles me.'

'She's a writer, Michael. And I daresay she's happy enough.'

'I chose him,' Liz said.

'Well, there you are then. It takes all sorts,' Olga chuckled.

One Christmas, the boys, as Monica liked to call us, gatecrashed a BBC fancy-dress party, arriving when things were just beginning to kick off. In the mêlée, two newsroom copy-takers were weaving about dressed as slave girls and belly-dancers, or a middle-class Anglo-Saxon version of it.

'You know what this is,' Ken said, smoking his pipe and clenching his fist on what to a Dexter drinker was the ultimate depravity, a glass of lager. 'This is nothing but a façade, that's what this is.'

Shortly after, he was knocked off his chair and fell to the floor. Not one drop of his drink was spilled. In another part of the chaos, Michael was interrogating a girl who had come as Sally Bowles.

'You're a nice lass,' he leered. 'And there's plenty of you. But what I want to know, did you 'ave to come in a bowler hat?'

'And who have you come as?'

'I have come as Frank Sinatra, darling.'

In his days as a cinema projectionist, he had spent two years perfecting a Rachmaninov run up and down the keys of a piano, without otherwise being able to pick out the tune to 'Three Blind Mice'. It was his party trick. He would open up the host's piano, play a faultless thirty-second glissando and then close the lid with a knowing and regretful shake of the head. There is hardly a day passes when I don't think about this and the huge pleasure it gave. Barstow could not have done it, nor Michael's other literary god, Hemingway.

He wrote half a dozen radio plays before he died and was that invaluable asset to any friendship, a reliable witness. All four of them were. We knew a great many better-connected people, closer by far to the world of ideas but none so simple and straightforward, so rooted in expressive common sense.

'You indulge them,' Liz chided.

'They indulge us. We know a lot about a lot of things but not enough about what they know. Without trying. And that's the key.'

I proposed, and they accepted, a weekend in Paris.

As the plane taxied at Manchester, Olga, who had never flown before, caught the sleeve of a cabin attendant.

'I don't want to cause a panic, love, but if you look out the window, you'll see the wing is just about to fall off.'

'Oh, it's designed to flex like that.'

'Is it? Well, it don't seem all that safe to me.'

Paris confused them. In Montmartre, I found them a 1930s bar with a neon-lit ceiling and suitably scruffy furniture, such as furnished many a location for Simenon. It was exactly the kind of place where a weary Maigret might stand himself and the nervy and stage-struck Lapointe a glass of white wine at the wrong hour of the day, before phoning Mme Maigret to tell her he would not be home for supper that night. Perhaps I made too much of all this: Olga was caught scowling. She held the fly-blown sandwich menu in her hand, looking underwhelmed.

'I would like something off this thing here before we go traipsing about any more.'

'Good idea. What do you fancy?'

'None of it's in English, Brian.'

A little later, I asked her how she was getting on with her *Sandwich du Jambon de Paris*.

'All it is, is ham between two slices of the bread that they have over here,' she replied grimly.

'It is a bit of a hellhole,' Liz murmured. 'I think we should divide our forces and meet up somewhere later on.'

Olga chose Notre Dame and was shepherded away by Ken and Monica.

'Bloody hell, we'll never see them again,' Michael muttered. He, Liz and I caught a cab to the Pompidou but at the escalators he spooked like a nervous horse. 'You go and have a look round, Liz, while me and our kid wait for you in that café there.'

Earlier in the day we had taken him to the Shakespeare and Company bookshop, to honour the memory of Ernest Hemingway. I did not tell him that this was not the original shop but a recreation of the Sylvia Beach site in the rue de l'Odéon. The story he wanted to hear was how Hemingway had 'liberated' Sylvia Beach, interrupting a cup of tea with her to attack some German snipers on the roofs nearby and then set off in his jeep to expropriate the wine cellars of the Ritz Hotel. All of which he listened to with glum attention. He had his ideas of the literary life and I had mine. Now he sat drinking red wine, looking faintly French in a battered corduroy jacket and wearing his flat cap low over his eyes. If he scowled, it was to convey deep thoughts about love and literature. At last he rose and waved his arms to explain who we were.

'*Los dos scribleros!*' he cried, to the amazement of the clientele, mostly Americans and Scandinavians.

On the return journey to England we drove like the wind from the airport to catch last orders at the Dexter. Olga declared she had had a lovely time. Someone asked her if I had been a reliable guide.

'No, he were bloody useless,' she explained cheerfully enough.

Who they were and the great pleasure they gave always reminds me of a classic line from a Sheffield panto. The Baron and the Principal Boy are bantering in a front-of-curtain routine when Dandini suddenly claps her hand to her ear, slaps her thigh and exclaims:

'A piano in this wood by chance
So now's the time for song and dance!'

5

Lady of the Lavender Mist

Liz's first novel had been written from a kneeling position in the matrimonial bedroom, typed on a venerable Remington which was balanced (of course) on a stool looted from Westminster Abbey on the occasion of the present Queen's wedding. I had been writing off and on for radio and television for ten years before I took it up as a living. Liz had a slight edge on me: she had learned to type at a West London secretarial college, from which had followed some disastrous engagements as a teenage personal assistant, or office dogsbody. Her typing was speedy but wildly inaccurate. But this led in turn to the necessity for filing and, by extension, an office of some kind. I once asked her where she had kept the drafts of her early writing, after the master of the house had come in from the bath.

'Under the bed,' she replied. 'After all, whoever looks under a bed?'

'And now you have a real office.'

'We both do.'

Hers faced into the road, where she was observed by the lady opposite.

'My word but you take some care over the shopping lists,' this guileless woman declared. 'I see you at it all day long.'

My own place was at the back of the house. There was nothing to look at through the window, which is always a good thing in an office. The work surface was a white melamine plank, supported at each end by two filing cabinets which doubled as wastepaper baskets. Mrs Wiggins was at a loss how to clean up the mess I created, most times peering around the door with an encouraging smile and leaving it at that. It confused her that we were not married, and I was known to her as Mr Um-Ar, the family supernumerary.

'A few flowers or a pot plant might cheer the place up a bit, Mr Um-ar. And do open the window from time to time. The smoke in here is something cruel.'

'I am writing about the First World War, Mrs Wiggins.'

'I know,' she said with great compassion. 'Mrs North says you are up to your hips in it. Well, you have it to do, I suppose.'

We were an unusual couple but no more so than our neighbours and friends. We gave no dinner parties but were invited to eat from time to time with Liz's old set, which included Margaret M., who liked people to wear dinner jackets and say interesting things about writers and painters who had forsaken God and were paying a dreadful price for it. These hospitable evenings were never returned, partly because we had no money and – much more starkly – because Liz described herself as 'all cooked out'. Her stand-by recipe was something called Orange Stew, the colour of which was dictated by a tin of tomato soup. (On the other hand, in thirty-seven years

together, we never cooked a thing which did not start
– however haphazardly – without frying up onions and
garlic.)

We read very different books. I had the habit of
buying market-stall non-fiction in an attempt to educate
myself beyond the limitations of the Cambridge English
Tripos. Liz was at the beginning of an encyclopaedic
knowledge of contemporary women's fiction. Once read,
never forgotten.

'Oh yes, her third book – but perhaps a bit baggy
compared to the others, don't you think? The young girl
is a memorable character, though. Brian is reading Frank
Jellinek on the Paris Commune, by the way.'

'Is he interested in French history?'

'Well, last week he was reading something called *Ice
Ages Great and Small*.'

'You say he watches television a lot.'

'Only to shout at it.'

'Where is he tonight?'

'Granada TV. They're recording something he wrote for
a series called *Send in the Girls*.'

Was that the night I was walking back to the Midland
Hotel with the actor and jazz singer Annie Ross when she
asked me what my favourite tune was? I said it was Duke
Ellington's 'Lady of the Lavender Mist'. To my delight
and astonishment, she stopped in her tracks and sang it
to me. Until that moment, I had no idea the tune had
lyrics.

'You have changed my life,' I said, seizing her hands.

'Is that your best shot?' Miss Ross asked drily. 'You're
a very easy boy to please.'

In these early years, I went to India to write and voice

a documentary about the railways. In the Nilgiri Hills, I glimpsed a vast sprawling bungalow of a place where we both might live and write the kind of books we were perhaps destined to write. It was another demonstration of my unrealistic expectations of what a writer's career might offer, a little tongue of flame easily doused by Liz's common sense.

'This is a place you saw from a train?'

'The series is called *Great Railway Journeys*.'

'Yes, but you didn't actually go round this place. You don't have a photograph and you haven't a clue of how to get there by car. You've just spent half an hour telling me about how your pipe and tobacco were stolen by monkeys in some Mysore palace. And how the only naked girl you saw in the time you were there was dead in the gutter outside the Taj Hotel being eaten by rats. These are cheesy advertisements for the sort of thing you're proposing.'

'But I also told you about the last surviving white member of the Ootacamund Club. Where the rules of snooker were laid down. A man after your own heart. A member of the warrior class. GSO2 Trieste in his day.'

'All very fascinating. But not enough.'

'Foreign parts, Elizabeth.'

'I haven't finished with Britain yet. I haven't *started* on Britain.'

Only a little while before this, she had set out to drive my youngest son to the station. Absorbed by a bit of plot in her work-in-progress, she had plunged ten miles into the Vale of York and delivered him to Thomas's prep school. He was too polite to point out her mistake and I always tell this story as a sign of her real affection for my children. She liked the boys but put even greater store by my daughter Clare.

'The man who gets her is going to be very lucky.'

'He'll certainly get an education out of her.'

'That is what women are for. To educate men. You hadn't noticed?'

The house filled up with books; the two offices did their duty. I began to get interesting commissions – including, in the end, seven stage plays, three of them for Alan Ayckbourn's Scarborough company, directed by the great man himself. In the first of these productions, the male lead was taken by John Arthur. Alan had already warned me not to attend rehearsals because it was a great irritation to the actors. I might come to the technical run, just in case there was a problem. John Arthur had what in conventionally staged theatre would be called the curtain speech.

'I've lived in this twon all my life and I can tell you, it's a twon without a soul,' he declared.

In the dark of the auditorium, I was galvanised, not to say agonised. I felt I had to say something. I spoke from a dry throat.

'Um, that speech contains a literal. The actual word is "town".'

'Is it? D'you know, I've always wondered what a sodding twon was.'

Alan smiled beatifically.

An uneasy truce existed with Liz's children. Thomas was now making his own wine, the premier cru being something labelled Elderberry, Banana, etc, which he sold to impressionable Stowe juniors. Sophie was painting and making sculptures. Philippa lived in New Mexico. Jo was at Edinburgh, living in what she described as Buckley-Ogh Street. Of my own children, Clare ended up in Germany, Peter in Ivy-League America and Steve in Brighton, playing jazz guitar for a living. As for ourselves, we adopted a life of uncomplaining obscurity, which would have been the same if we had shifted to literary London, or the mystery house in India.

The plain truth was that, for differing reasons, we were not ruthless enough to be writers of the first rank. Liz had the better chance but was almost wilfully negligent about publishing as a business. One of the pleasures to be got from writing fiction is that you can go to live in the world you have created. Liz was an extreme example of this. She wrote and rewrote obsessively, never quite able to let the last draft stand. As for me, I only too readily accepted that television, which was where the money came from, was a great hole in the ground that could never be filled. Accordingly, there was work for almost anybody. Once or twice a year a plum fell into my lap – an interesting commission or the stunning value added to the text by gifted and sympathetic actors. But these moments were all too fugitive.

One night the playwright and friend Hugh Whitemore and I were driving about in Battersea looking for what he called a respectably run off-licence when an elderly drunk swayed off the pavement and fell in front of the car. I jumped out, took off my jacket and put it under the man's head. As an afterthought, I took out his false teeth which were hanging loose in his mouth. Hugh joined me.

'I should make it clear, sir, that the man who is attending you is not a doctor but a not-very-well-known television playwright from the North of England.'

'Bugger me,' the drunk cried piteously. 'I never had no luck, not since I come out the army.'

Liz and I were each busy in our different ways but at heart inward-looking, which is to say (perhaps) too wrapped up in each other. We were, we hoped, that elusive quantity, a contented couple. The relationship was by no means without its own shocks and setbacks but she took it for granted that I would bring in enough money to keep the lights on; and I took it that as long as we stayed together, we could come to no harm.

But then there is this, from her novel *Worldly Goods*, published in 1987. It is the thinly disguised account of the marriage of Elizabeth to David Howard. Just before the wedding, Nina-Elizabeth is waiting for Campbell-David:

> Before dark, she decided that instead of listening for Campbell's car she would go down to the beach, one of the best places that she knew to be alone. She was better at being alone than she was at being with other people, which may have been yet another reason for marrying Campbell. She'd been out with several young men and they, like Campbell, talked a lot about themselves and their experiences. Nina would sit there listening, but would not in fact be listening. Eventually they would realise this and not ask her out again. Campbell was different: he didn't notice when she wasn't listening.

Maybe that was it. Maybe we were happy together because I never noticed when she wasn't listening.

6

Telling Us Apart

A few months after writing the first pages of this book, I was crossing the appropriately named Old Road to catch a bus when I stumbled and stretched my length. I hit the tarmac on the crown of the carriageway without being able to defend my fall and broke my nose, possibly a rib and certainly a bone in my foot. I was dragged to safety by a wonderfully quick-witted passer-by called Susan who sat me against a crumbling yellow wall and phoned for an ambulance. There was a gratifying amount of blood on my face and chest. The paramedic who attended asked me my address and whether there was anyone at home who could care for me.

'Maybe he is homeless,' a bystander suggested in an effort to be helpful.

'I don't think so,' Susan said, reaching for my hand. Some of the warmth in my beard was blood and some tears.

'I live alone,' I mumbled.

It was of course an unsatisfactory and even a dishonest answer, for though Liz will never come back through that blue front door, inside me her presence persists, as real to me as my own existence. When I turn the key in the lock, she is always right behind me. If I have been out on my own, I have acquired the habit of walking to the window to see whether she is in the garden. How to explain this to people who tell me the pain will one day pass? Love – and loss – is not tied with a satin bow but a series of granny knots.

After the accident I spent three and a half hours waiting in A & E and was given five minutes of cursory examination. A jolly nurse asked me if I had sobered up. In a fit of sulks I refused to wait another hour for an X-ray and discharged myself. I caught a cab home and fell into a sofa to tell Liz all about it, just as if she were there. She asked me what kind of a doctor I had seen and when I described him as an irritating little twerp, she laughed. It was worth a broken rib to hear that abrupt and sudden laughter once again, the unchanged thing she had brought with her from childhood. It came as if from a photograph taken in the gardens of the Admiral's Residence, Gibraltar. She is a skinny child posed in a Royal Marine pith helmet, a drum around her neck, sticks at the ready. She looks defensive and also truculent, as though the capturing of the image is a favour demanded by the adult world. This is a child that rarely throws her head back in delight but, when egged on by the naval rating assigned to look after her, might produce that same sudden tee-hee staccato.

In 1982, her novel *Ancient Enemies* was published to great critical acclaim. The storyteller and central character is a sixteen-year-old schoolgirl trying to interpret her mother's second marriage to the barely likeable Henry. The book is a funny and exasperating view of adult life told by a very unreliable witness and – because it is written by a fictionalist of great compassion – there lurks underneath a hidden river of tragedy. What makes Petra unforgettable is that she knows nothing about love. What makes the tragedy is that perhaps she never will.

Ancient Enemies is fairly easy to deconstruct, though some of Liz's most mordant wit can be found in the subtlety of the disguises and sleights of hand within it. (There are people characterized in the book – that is to say, family members and friends – who have yet to recognise themselves). But for me what made the novel such uncomfortable reading was the portrait of Petra's mother, who is represented as a silly, vacillating woman wounded by love, struck down by it. The self-regarding and feckless Henry is the object of her desire but even such a shallow person as he can bring her to abject misery. It was only much later that I realized what had upset me was in reality a sublime double bluff. This was not she, nor did she know anyone remotely like the character she depicted. The woman who lived in our house and read *Thomas the Tank Engine* to the grandchildren in such cut-glass diction was at pains to make The Fat Controller a woman, all the more alluring for being invisible.

'Then who is the man in the top hat, Granny?'

'Oh, just some pushy fat man – you know the sort. I suppose you need a man to do all the play-acting. Waggling flags and blowing whistles. But the brains of the business is a woman. Obviously.'

In appearance she was a little below her wished-for height, with chunky wrists and short hands inherited from her father, who to my mind much resembled the once-famous character actor, Robertson Hare, whose catchphrase was 'O Calamity!'. She was one of those lucky women who inspire confidence in other women – her dress sense was much admired, all the more so for being inimitable. When she was in her late thirties, she took a mature degree in English and Philosophy at Leeds University. Her jeans were fashionably distressed but she wore them with incredibly expensive boots and collarless muslin shirts. My own clothes were minor variants of what I had worn at Cambridge twenty years earlier, but Liz understood the butterfly flight of fashion. It was a joy to see her marching down the steps of the Parkinson Building, hugging her books, her expression blanked out by huge Sophia Loren sunglasses. It was an image to set at odds with the *Tatler* photograph of her taken shortly after she came out at Court, where she looks (in tune with the times) commendably vacuous and apparently carved from lard. The print was stuffed in a drawer and only produced at Christmas time to tease her into howls of anguish. It was a picture of someone who had ceased to exist.

She knew the Cole Porter and Irving Berlin songbooks back to front. Her list of favourite vocalists was short but eclectic: Jacques Brel, Charles Trenet, Tony Bennett, Frank Sinatra; but also Ian Dury, Gloria Gaynor, Paolo Conte and (alas) George Formby. She was a Grade Eight pianist and a childhood ukelele player. None of these enthusiasms were written on her sleeve. She had to have them winkled out of her, as for example when someone at a party, in an effort to ingratiate himself, said something disparaging about Barry Manilow.

'Just at the moment, I can't think of anyone I'd rather be,' Liz rejoined, her tiny jaw jutting.

She loved crosswords, acrostics, numerical codes, Sudoku and every form of paper game. She played bridge with expressionless ferocity, studied the stars and – as was to be proved – spoke impeccable French. Her dancing borrowed heavily from the sailor's hornpipe. Just how much of all this hinterland was evident to people younger than herself is hard to judge, just as her dedication to the craft of fiction could be reinterpreted as some form of heightened absent-mindedness. One of her siblings found a way of putting all this: regrettably and to the shame of the family, she was just trying to be clever.

She was in fact fighting something inside herself. There was a deeply buried spiritual melancholy in Liz that nothing could eradicate. Her fruitless and self-harming battles with her former husband were a sign of it and it only gradually dawned on me that having a merry-Andrew as replacement could be just as vexing. A woman, if she is to survive, must have the art of dissembling her deepest feelings. These were beyond my reach, as they had been for David. She was not trying to be clever. She was trying to hide.

For nearly twenty years of our time in Yorkshire we threw a New Year's Eve party, when Apollo went out the window and – for one night only – Dionysius made himself at home. In this we were egged on by the doyen of radio drama producers, Alfred Bradley. Alfred was incurably merry, with the additional genius of being able to animate an entire houseful of guests on three halves of lager. His tailor was Marks and Spencer and thus in appearance he resembled a knowing and faintly venal Roman senator dressed in baby-blue lambswool. Alfred knew everybody. He had dozens of wonderful green-room stories and was a reckless gossip. He commended the idea of living in France but understood the potential cost to Liz.

'I should think it's just about the last place to be given your space. All that kissing and handshaking. You should have made him buy you a cottage in Norway. With only the cod for neighbours.'

'It's his dream, not mine.'

'But that's it. You don't dream, do you?' he smiled.

'I do. Of course I do. But I don't feel I can go about telling everybody.'

'That's what makes you so formidable.'

'Brian's always using that word about me.'

All this while a gate-crashing poet had been patiently assembling the bits and pieces of a one-man band. He staggered about with a surly expression, festooned with cymbals and wires, a little red drum strapped to his back, waiting to be invited to play, yet utterly disregarded by the people around about him.

'Go ahead,' Alfred encouraged him. 'All the music lovers are in the other room.'

In the other room, Jokke Cryer had fallen backwards into a bowl of trifle and Michael Toft was having his annual consultation with the Wetherby coroner, on the subject of how he could be certain that overworked hospital doctors would not nail him into a coffin while he was still alive. Nearby, the secretary of the Harrogate Branch Labour Party, the wholly worthy Val Smith, had recently won a national poetry competition and wanted to celebrate with someone.

'It's about fellatio,' she explained giddily to Anita Mason. 'What do you think?'

There was a clue to the probable answer in Anita's motorcycle jacket and severely cut black jeans, her cropped hair and Belmondo rollie.

'Dunno,' she shrugged. 'Never tried it.'

There was always a family inquest on New Year's Day, at which an attempt was made to draw together the flirtations and conversational pratfalls of so many drunken guests. A young solicitor who had played amateur football for England at Wembley had clashed with Sophie just short of fisticuffs. Philippa's American husband had whimsically stuffed his finger down the neck of an Eric Stockl pot and then found he could not get it out. Jo's rock-climbing boyfriend, who had run five miles over the tops to be present, took on an academic from York about the doubtful value of a university education – and so on.

'Sid knows all there is to know about gunshot injuries. A transverse wound to the buttocks will always provide buckets of blood without proving fatal.'

'Who was the man who looked like Pete Morgan?'

'The Earl of Harewood'.

'Try not to be funny.'

'It was Pete Morgan, you dope.'

'Ken never left the kitchen all night. He was talking to Mummy for ages about how you don't find many public clocks about these days, or not as many as you used to.'

'The one-man-band poet was thoroughly pissed off.'

'Because Alfred asked him to play the "Dead March" from *Saul*.'

'No, because he called him the last of the cymbalists.'

'The poor man was only trying to get Alfred to commission him.'

'Work,' Liz said wearily. 'There is only work. That's all that matters. Everything else is fancy dress.'

'But what about the one-man band? Isn't that a clever form of disguise?' I asked.

'There is no such thing as a one-man band,' she replied, searching me with her wonderful grey eyes. 'You know that.'

It used to be my occasional complaint that though we talked incessantly, we didn't talk enough.

'What rubbish. We talk all the time. You hardly ever stop talking. You do have these occasional spells where for three or four days you won't talk to *anyone* and you may have noticed how panicky that makes me feel.'

'You're not bored?'

'Not particularly. Is it France we're talking about?'

'Or not talking about.'

'France is fine. I'm fine with France.'

'You think you'll be able to work there?' I asked.

'I doubt it. I shall make lots of notes, though.'

'Isn't that work?'

She thought about it and shrugged. We studied each other.

'I feel unsettled, if that's what you're trying to get out of me. France is a side issue. After all, if we do go, we're not moving there for good. At least, I hope not.' She looked into her eye's reflection shimmering in a mug of camomile tea and then levelled a rare unsmiling stare at me. 'Tell me, forgetting France for the moment, would you ever consider leaving Yorkshire?'

'Name the day,' I said shakily.

It was something she had never before mentioned. The wreckage of the New Year's Eve party was still all around us – sticky glasses, empty bottles, plates of potato salad garnished with cigarette ends, books dragged down from the shelves and left to flounder. Somebody's camera, a set of keys.

'How long have you felt unsettled?'

'Oh, come off it. You know what I'm talking about. We've done Yorkshire. We've made a handful of really good friends and you – of course – a regiment of enemies. Let's just say we need to turn a page.'

'Where next, then?'

'Well, nearer the Channel ports for a start. A city, not a village. Not a city either. A leafy lane suburb within level walking distance of some shops. A decent garden. And a clean slate.'

'You think there's still a clean slate left in us?'

'I want the same-old same-old for us, of course I do, but with different landscapes. Different air.'

'Which is where France comes in,' I suggested hopefully.

'Have you ever lived in a village?' she flashed back. 'You want me to yourself, that's what this is really about.'

'Is that so bad?'

'It frightens me.'

Of course it did. The night before, in the mêlée that ushered in the New Year, we had hardly time to talk to each other. As midnight chimed, I kissed half a dozen women before finding her behind a door, talking in the gravest terms to Val Smith about the Labour Party. I knew how much it cost her to nuance a dozen or more conflicting conversations like this, a thing she thought she was bad at but for which, after she died, she would be especially fondly remembered. She had the gift of intelligent listening.

What she was afraid of most was becoming an expatriate in experience and temperament. By this time there were grandchildren, both here and in America. She followed their progress in the closest detail, but always with a writer's eye. They could do no wrong, yet changed nothing. They were part of the flux of existence and while she was there to provide them with a sentimental view of dotty old granny, their real purpose was to make her think. In so far as a family is a collection of discrete families and their fortunes, Liz's affection for her grandchildren was genuine and all-embracing. It was how things hung together. They were part of a great fiction, of which she was presently the caretaker author. In time these same children would perhaps write their own novels, on the same theme – a family and its loyalties. It was an idea that fascinated her.

In the meantime, there were things she did not insist on with her grandchildren but was careful to mention as important. Everyone should read the King James' version of the Bible. They should know half a dozen hymns by heart and as many poems. The words to the 'Marseillaise' were bracing and you could not go far wrong with the Band of the Royal Marines. Piercings and tattoos were mere vulgar ostentation, as was the government front bench. The unexamined life was not worth living, as Socrates had testified at his trial. Finally, there could hardly have been a better man in all creation than the actor Peter Finch.

*   *   *

We returned to France at the beginning of August. It was an incredibly hot day and we were exhausted by the journey. To save money we crossed Newhaven–Dieppe, leaving us a long and vexing slog, not much solaced by Charles Trenet tapes and Cox's Orange Pippins. Half a year's telephone calls and letters to the builders had wrought some changes during our absence but the improvements were more like a form of mockery. There was an internal loo and bathroom – but no water. There was a *fosse d'étanche* buried in the yard, located by a preposterous stench pipe that stuck up two metres. Stairs to the upper floor were still in the workshop.

The situation called for swift and decisive Anglo-Saxon bad temper and the brutally foreign way of telling the time the English bring to living abroad. Or, as the French would say more economically, banging their palms together, it needed a little biff-boff. After one glance, we retreated to the Hôtel du Commerce and booked two rooms.

Our travelling companions were Paul and Callie, our neighbours in Yorkshire. They were heading for Cibourne, where they would meet up with Jill and Graham in front of Ravel's birthplace. Paul was a violinist and Callie a cellist and together they represented 50 per cent of the Leeds String Quartet. He was famous for his impetuous enthusiasms, both musical and otherwise. One of these was cycling, a thing he hardly ever did in England but practised recklessly in France. I think, left to himself, he would have cycled down to the Basque country in his vest and lime-green running shorts. He found Charente Maritime appealingly flat but was exasperated by the local habit that car drivers had of zipping past cyclists with only a few centimetres to spare. The toot they gave as they passed was in the nature of a sardonic greeting as well as the French way of expressing solidarity with other road users.

Callie was calmer and more pragmatic. She liked food and worshipped the sun. She cherished small events and fleeting moments. Time moved slowly for Callie, while for Paul it rushed by in a torrent, leaving him to cycle furiously in an attempt to catch up. We had spent holidays together in Paxos for three or four years. There, Callie lay topless on the pebbles; Paul swam out to sea several hundred yards, his black head bobbing. The French found virtue in them both. One was a character from opera-bouffe, the other an odalisque. One came from the *caserne* at a high trot, tooting a trumpet, the other lay in a sixth-floor attic bed, watching the sun cross the ceiling and waiting for something (maybe someone) to turn up.

'I saw M. Paul this morning, very early, cycling to Siecq.'

'He was taking the empties to the bottle-bank.'

'But at seven in the morning?'

'It is his way.'

However, in such a situation as we found ourselves, Paul was at his best. The day after our arrival we took down the cupboard in which Gaston had kept his single plate, his saucepan and other useful bits and pieces – twine, empty soup tins, porcelain fuse blocks and one or two rose-red oblongs which turned out to be ancient razor blades. Then he and I set about demolishing a dividing wall in the *salle de séjour*, one that was built out of hollow red fireclay blocks. Bashing things was balm to his soul. Throwing the debris out of the window was just as therapeutic.

Callie began hacking plaster from the end wall in silent

self-absorption. The idea – my idea – was to create an effect seen in many banks and offices – a naked wall described by the French as *les pierres apparentes*. But what was appearing were limestone chunks in wavering courses and not, as I had imagined, beautifully dressed masonry to please the eye and tease the imagination.

'I was too hot,' Liz wrote in her notebook. 'Sat under a barn roof (missing grass and trees) and hoping for a breeze.'

This defection had not gone unnoticed. The tension was broken by the arrival of the dentist Pierre Milhat, crisp in a white shirt and pearl-grey slacks. He had a suggestion to make. It had come to him in the middle of an extraction. We should knock down the cow byre and at least two of the three barns. It was all so simple! M. Dieumegard, whose tooth he had pulled that very morning, was building a farm road and could be persuaded to demolish the barns and cart away the rubble for nothing. Liz practically fell on his neck.

'Wouldn't that be marvellous?'

'Yes, but –'

Pierre rounded on me with a cheery laugh. 'You are always saying "yes, but". Look what you've done in one morning! You now have a *salle de séjour* five metres square. Soon you will have a walled garden, the envy of all your neighbours. Soon enough, trees, um, a barbeque pit, maybe a pool. Paul and Callie can bring out their students to play for the locals, bringing fame and culture to the commune.'

'Yes,' Paul cried. 'The Shostakovich, Callie!'

Callie stood with a scarf knotted over her blonde hair, her skin coated with dust and a fireman's axe loose in her hand. Her face was white with dust, all save her nose, which was pink from scuffing.

'Who is your favourite composer?' she asked Pierre.

'Schubert.'

Next day, we were visited by Mère Pasquet. It had been her habit for many years to walk down the road when the heat of the sun was waning, from a time when the roadway itself was mud and dust and the traffic comprised carts and occasional tractors. She walked in the middle of the road because that had always been her way. Nowadays she was passed on both sides by huge lorries and speeding cars but had no fear of them. This little old lady, her feet stuffed into check slippers, had something of the duchess about her. She had the gift of containment, which extended to her speech and address. She was still extraordinarily beautiful and must have been ravishing as a young woman. We offered her a camping chair which she inspected and declined. Her pale blue eyes studied us.

'I live with my daughter nowadays,' she said at last.

'Were you born in the village, Madame?'

She pointed her stick at a corner of the room.

'This was your *maison natale*?'

'Gaston was my brother.'

'He was much-loved, people have told us.'

'That is so,' she confirmed.

'We did not know you were born here,' Liz said.

'That was a long time ago. I am still quite well but I suffer from *un peu de vertige*. You have an honest face,' she added, unsmilingly. 'Do you have children?'

'Four.'

'They can be a comfort. What do they do?'

'One lives in America. One is a painter, an artist. One works in an office. One is a chef, or at least a sous-chef.'

Mère Pasquet shrugged. She pursed her lips in the way people do who could not care less about the answer they have just been given. A long silence followed.

'Gaston had some chairs that I have kept in store. Perhaps you should have them.'

'That would be wonderful.'

'You speak very correct French. Are you from Paris?'

'We are English, Madame.'

The corners of her mouth moved upwards a millimetre or so. She had made a joke. Another thought occurred to her. 'There is a club for people of the *troisième âge*. I am inscribed, of course. But there's little in it for me. I am too old.'

'Madame Elizabeth will join the ranks of the *troisième âge* this year,' I said.

'Is that true?' Mme Pasquet asked her.

'In a fortnight. But I do not like to be reminded of it.'

'It happens.'

Once more she pointed with her stick to the far corner of the room.

'I was born there. In the dark, I suppose.'

And for the first time she smiled – briefly, but with such graciousness that it took my breath away.

'May I walk you back to your house?' I asked.

'That is kind, *m'sieu*. But I am not lost.'

'Madame,' Liz said. 'We are thinking about pulling down two of the barns.'

'Why do you tell me?'

'It will make a big difference. I shall see trees. But for you, perhaps –'

'It is your house now,' Mère Pasquet said, as if to a child. 'You are too polite, madame. I have heard this said about the English. Some of them.'

She raised her stick in farewell and – walking out into the middle of the road – set off back up the hill.

House Warming

It never once crossed my mind to write about France while we lived there, either in a descriptive way or in a linking narrative such as might make a play, or a novel. If anything, I was there in search of a pleasure dome, where I could practise at being someone I was not. There was a journal kicking about the house, intended for loftier thoughts and reflections but much more often used as a place for handy telephone numbers, sketch plans for improvements that never came to fruition; more vitally, for the arrival dates of visitors from England. Liz's contributions were recipes for dishes she had no intention of cooking, dictated to her by kindly neighbours; and lists of vocabulary and plants. From May to September, we wrote nothing that could earn us a single penny. This did not go unnoticed in London, where the money was.

In the first television play I ever wrote (in time stolen from a full-time job in education and long before I did it for a living), I learned an early lesson in how the medium worked. I was still very green and came to the studios utterly without what you might call writers' linen. I wore my one good suit and a blue wool tie. I was, if you want to put it this way, a civilian. (Mike Toft turned up for his first day as a face worker at Shillington Colliery in a sports jacket and tie. His mam had sponged and ironed his flannels. I did not feel any less awkward.) The director was a pattern professional as to dress – jeans, faded blue denim shirt and the most amazingly distressed suede boots. In the fifth or sixth scene he suddenly threw his cigarettes at the gallery window and howled like a wolf at the ceiling, asking it what on earth it was that had given an actress the idea that she had a talent for the work.

'I'm going down onto the floor to talk to her,' he said.

The mikes were up on the set and I watched entranced as he ran and embraced this poor woman. This is what he said: 'What you're doing is blinding, dear heart, absolutely blinding. No, I really mean it. But the script is so bloody awful, I'm afraid you're going to have to act it.'

She was not stupid: her head jerked back as if she had been struck. When he came back up to the gallery, he walked straight to me and kissed me on the forehead.

'It's not a story about you,' he said. 'It's just television.'

He plumped himself down in front of the desk in a chair that sighed as deeply as he.

'It's only television,' he muttered.

After more than ten years of such adventures, I eventually wrote a stage play about the business, called *Turning Over*. It was produced at the Bush Theatre, half a mile from BBC Television Centre, from where it drew many of its audience. The plot – as much of it as there was – concerned the making of a travel documentary in India.

'In the presence of this melancholy bygone,' the grave and noble Mr Mehta intones, waving his arm to indicate an imaginary temple, 'we are forced to examine this question: "why are we here?"' He waggles his head from side to side with a gentle smile. 'That is to say, not to ask why are we here. But here.'

'What a great question!' I made the breezy director croon. 'So. All we need now is a few little wordies to give it the old razzmatazz. That wry thing you're so good at.'

'Is wry good?'

'It's gold dust, mate. Wry, quizzical, all that educated shit.'

In another part of the play the unhappy and bewildered writer tries to characterize the director for the benefit of a beautiful woman. 'He was at a Poly, you know, studying philosophy and tap-dancing. And failed the philosophy.'

It happened one night that Harold Pinter and his wife were in to see the show. Lady Antonia laughed politely at this line, but Harold turned and examined me with a baleful stare. Was I going to be political at last? Or was I going to persevere with all this wry and quizzical shit?

Our immediate neighbours in France lived in an adjoining house that had once been the village shop. The wall that separated our courtyards was three metres high and the family lived in seclusion behind tall wooden gates. They were a young couple with two children – civil but extremely cautious. (We found out later that the husband, Jean-Yves, had made a bid for our house and had it turned down.)

He was a blond giant, normally dressed in green dungarees and most often glimpsed on tractors or driving three-decker threshing machines past the house on his way to distant fields. Ghislaine, his wife, was dark-eyed and dark-haired – her business was with goats. The milk was sold to a cooperative.

Jean-Yves was a farmer without land of his own who worked all the hours God sent for an agri-businessman, one of whose massive maize fields faced our own house. This man's wife was the agent to an insurance company. They were, accordingly, a step up from the ordinary, one instance of which was how seldom they were seen anywhere on foot. They buzzed about in newish cars, no doubt grinding their teeth when encountering Mme Pasquet tottering along the crown of the road in front of them. Like me, they came from somewhere else and had no family connections in the area. Jean-Yves worked for this couple as that most prized of things (and ultimate French compliment), *un homme sérieux*.

Much that had once been in the village had gone – the village shop, the small family farms (and with them their horses and tractors), the football team, the *gardien des champs*, who in the day had patrolled the fields wearing his official brassard. The two *maisons bourgeoises*, one of which now belonged to holiday-making Parisians, were no longer staffed by servants nor their summer lawns populated by elegant women and comfortably mousta-chioed men. In the second of these houses a tattered moth of a woman persisted, a daughter who had been robbed of her fiancé in the Great War and outlived everyone else in the family to occupy the place on her own, living in one room. The village school was on its last legs. Soon the children under eleven – and there were only six of them – would be bussed to Macqueville, five kilometres away. Riffault, the postman, did his rounds in a yellow van, with the entire day's delivery for our hamlet on the passenger seat beside him, maybe two dozen letters and circulars. There was a common phrase for all that had come to pass. We were a *village triste*.

The first French interior we entered belonged to the ebullient Mme Ayraud, widowed by the medical disaster that befell her husband after what should have been a routine blood transfusion. Paulette Ayraud came from Paris originally. Her father was a ticket collector on the Métro and when the Germans arrived in 1940 the tenement in which the family lived was requisitioned. They fled, but only a little way from Paris the train was commandeered by the SS. In the confusion, Paulette was separated from her parents and walked south on her own. She was twelve years old. Somehow or other, she reached what I had already begun to think of as 'our' commune and began life all over again as a fieldworker. In time she married her employer, lucky man.

'Watch out for the Parisians,' she said within an hour of meeting us. 'We have a family of them across the road, who come for three weeks in the summer. The wife, I think she is, has asked us to do something about the cows, who shit on the road when they're driven out to pasture. The Parisians don't like it. It makes the tyres on their cars dirty. "Well, my good woman," I said, "I will wipe their arses for you every morning with a good quality toilet paper. It will be a pleasure to make you happy."'

Paulette made so free and easy with us because she cottoned on at once to who we were. She had a quiverful of children and her seventh son lived in the original farmhouse with his wife and the ultra-polite Romain, the spindly legged grandson who was summoned by grandma to meet us. His mother, Martine, had married into the village from an office job forty or more kilometres away. She monitored her mother-in-law's comments with a wry smile.

'Will you bring workers over from England to help you renovate Gaston's house?' she asked politely. It was by way of being a trick question.

'We shall try to employ people locally,' Liz said.

'That is good to hear.'

'Pouf!' Paulette exclaimed. 'These English! Some of them arrive with two or three lorries loaded with stuff – cement, guttering, tiles, even. And they bring their own workers! To save them the trouble of speaking French! And what is the first thing they want? A swimming pool!'

'Or so people say,' Martine murmured.

'We are different,' I said. 'The first thing we need is trees.'

'Oh, *mon pauvre!* There is not a scrap of soil on that property. You'd be better off living in the woods,' Paulette cackled.

Her house, which had once perhaps been for farm servants, faced directly onto the cow manger. It was dark and crowded with little objects on every flat surface – china ornaments, photo frames, plaster shepherdesses and other holiday knickknacks garnered from the coast, where her daughter managed a nudist camp.

'That is interesting.'

'You'd think so. But believe me, taking your clothes off doesn't make you any happier than you were before.'

A huge television was playing with the sound down – Paulette was devoted to the afternoon soaps. Her picture of Britain was derived entirely from dubbed episodes of

The Avengers and the marital difficulties of Prince Charles and the glamorous Laddydee.

We sat at a table covered in chequered oilcloth and ate salty biscuits, washed down with pastis. A green plastic swat lay to hand, which was used on flies as big as blackberries. There was also a raddled old pug called Jalna wandering about in a state of confusion, drool dripping from her jaws. Paulette had only to show her the fly swat for her to retreat clumsily back out into the yard.

'And so. What do you make of Jean-Yves and Ghislaine?' she asked.

'Hush,' her daughter-in-law chided sharply.

'They won't like you coming round here.'

'That's enough!'

'Madame Ayraud,' Liz said gently. 'We cannot begin by taking sides. We cannot judge others in the village, *coûte qu'il coûte*. In short, we must try to be friends with everybody.'

Paulette fixed us both with a contrite smile. 'You're right. I talk too much.'

'Rest easy, madame. I am already very used to that,' Liz murmured, patting me on the head by way of explanation.

My horoscope for that day came from the regional newspaper *Le Sud-Ouest* and read, 'Social Life: You are trying too hard to be well thought of and making foolish errors. Bah! It's not too bad a fault and it won't cause you any grief. The Heart: Come down from your ivory tower and look around among your friends. They live in a different way. Health: What are you doing about your kidneys?'

'This is not fair commentary on Taureans. I would say

it applies better to certain badly aspected Leos. You, for example.'

'There is nothing wrong with my kidneys that a flush lavatory would not cure,' Liz said. 'Nor do I live in an ivory tower, as these lists I've been making demonstrate. They are basic peasant necessities.'

Top of the list was a fridge. We bought one from Mme Talon next day. She was a glamorous woman with a white goods store in Matha, a small town like many others in *la France profonde* that flattered only to deceive. Whatever had been in Matha was long gone, leaving behind a ridiculously imposing Hôtel de Ville and a few streets of fairly desperate shops. All the action was in the huge out-of-town supermarkets and their buzzing car parks. Paulette Ayraud had already recommended Mammouth to us, a massive retail outlet near Angoulême, thirty kilometres away. Her daughter-in-law drove her there once a fortnight.

'You never see the same people twice,' Paulette added helpfully.

Meanwhile the ubiquitous Milhat had mentioned our name to some of his cronies. In this way we were visited unexpectedly on a blowy day by Gilbert and Jacqueline Margerie, he formerly an art director for the movies, she an actress. Gilbert wore a Marks and Spencer's blazer and a blue cravat. His grey slacks were a poem. He inspected *les pierres apparentes* with deep dismay and recommended they be coated with something called *Chaux de St Astier*. When I had to break off these discussions to rescue an unstayed window from taking wing to Cognac, he smiled and changed tack, telling me of his adventures with Robert Mitchum on the shoot of *The Longest Day*.

'*Il était très sympa*,' he sighed.

'Mme Margerie looked very cold but said twice she was OK,' Liz scribbled in her notebook that night. 'Later in the visit I sat where she had been. Silly cow, it was horrible. Many stories were told, including Paul's about Rachmaninov and the cellist's coat, which requires translation and also benefits from translation. His wife tells me I have the sort of face that would catch the light for the camera. She had to say something, I suppose. He tells me I should send copies of my books to Disney.'

In other words, we were being gently tried out. We had a card of our own to play. Liz's composer brother gave up a beach holiday in Spain to come out to see us and try to be useful. Roger made a good impression, the more so because he looked and behaved in an impeccably English way – an elderly and self-effacing beardie wearing a ruined straw hat first purchased by his father fifty years earlier. His purple desert boots also attracted admiration. It helped that he was more than slightly deaf and had the pleasing habit of taking out his hearing aid when things got complicated (or boring) and laying it down regretfully on the table. Rene Boucherie liked him.

'How old is your father?' he whispered.

'What does he say?' Roger asked.

'That you cut a fine figure of a man.'

'Hardly likely,' the composer sniffed. 'I heard barely five notes, ending on an interrogation.'

We were invited to dinner *chez* Milhat, where we ate outdoors by candlelight, ten of us at table. Ranged against one wall was a woodpile. Every log was identical in size and each had been sprayed with a burgundy-coloured wood dye. It was impressive.

One of the guests was a gaunt and wild-eyed artist of quite extraordinary severity, whose opinion it was that only children knew how to paint. All the rest was flimflam.

'What about Matisse, however?'

'I detest Matisse,' this old man shouted.

I told the story of how friends had once tried to hypnotize the artist by asking to him to stare fixedly at a patterned carpet. After a few minutes, they asked him how he felt.

'I can still see the carpet,' he replied calmly.

It hardly set the table in a roar, but my secret intention was to attract the interest of the young companion the Matisse-detester had brought along, a stunningly beautiful Japanese girl in a grey silk blouse and huge black beach pyjamas.

'You don't listen so prop'ly,' she lisped in English. 'Matisse no good.'

Driving home, Roger chuckled gently. 'I'm not sure you were getting all your points across tonight.'

'I'm pretty certain Mme Milhat is having a thing with that hunk with the poetic black hair,' Liz mused from the back seat.

'Really? He looked a bit too obvious to me,' Roger sighed. 'But then I can't say I know much about adultery, in France or anywhere else come to that. If it's all right with you two, tomorrow I'll climb up into that attic sort of place you have above the *chai* and have a poke around. There might be an old table we can use.'

That night I lay beside Liz, horribly wide awake. I could not get Milhat's damned woodpile out of my mind and its ironic significance. These were people who had everything. From being a romantic gesture, buying our own house now

seemed merely a selfish act, leading to unforeseeable consequences. We had no money, I had no practical skills. Liz,
for all her long-suffering patience with me, was being asked
to give up (or at the very least adapt) her native caution
to furnish somebody else's shapeless dream. It occurred to
me, listening to a fox bark out in the woods, that we might
have started out like that from the moment we first met,
something very skilfully concealed from me. This was an
uncomfortable thought and in its way a kind of treason.

Until I blurted it out to Mme Pasquet, I had not thought
of Liz as being in her sixtieth year. For me, she was always
the glorious forty-year-old who had ghosted into my life
almost by accident. We still talked like the people we had
been then, used the same shorthand descriptions, enjoyed
the same films and landscape, colours and choice of wines.
And at dinner that night she shone as just that person,
lighting up the mauve and grey gloom of Milhat's courtyard in a white shirt and black satin trousers, a chiffon
scarf loosely knotted as a tie. I was already dismayed by
the unmistakable evidence that we were eating with people
who could – at any rate in France – buy us twice over.
Liz remained calm. Having, as he thought, seen me off,
the crazy artist turned his fire on her.

'I will go on to say that children, just as they paint
better, write better than adults,' he bellowed. The whole
table fell silent, waiting to hear how she would reply.

She lit a cigarette. 'I have never heard that said, *m'sieu*.'

'Then you must open your mind. Learn to think like a
child.'

'Your daughter is very beautiful. Is your wife Japanese?'

'She is not my daughter,' he said, furious. 'Everybody
here knows she is not my daughter.'

'A thousand apologies. I was trying to think like a child,' she explained, ignoring Milhat's hoot of laughter.

And it came to me, not for the first time, how unutterable love is, how every once in a while it breaks overhead, as if from another dimension altogether. In that one unimportant moment was compressed all the reasons to love her more completely than I have ever loved anyone. She was annoyed with herself for having lost her temper and I think doubly annoyed by having had her hand seized in admiration by the man sitting next to her. She smiled bleakly and picked up her glass, looking down the length of the table at me. Her expression seemed to be saying Look! I have given something of myself to these people that I did not intend to give. It's all too much. Your stuff about Matisse was enough. As for the Japanese girl, dream on.

Roger did not find a table next morning but did come down the ladder with a worm-eaten door. What else was it but a table-top with keyholes cut in it? The two siblings drove to Beauvais to buy trestles from a builder's yard owned by two brothers. One was quiet and attentive to business. The other was loud and exuberant. Later, in the tiny Co-op round the corner, Liz met a very remarkable woman called Dorothea Alcock. She and her husband lived in a *maison bourgeoise* at a place called Bazauges, a few kilometres to the north. They were retired, or, as the French have it, *en retraite*.

'I sort of invited them to come over the night of my birthday. He's called John and they both worked at Bletchley Park during the war. It wasn't until the sixties that they could tell their children what they'd been up to. You'll like them.'

'Shall we give them a meal?'

'I said drinks but then it occurred to me to make it early doors, so to speak, and invite the neighbours. We clearly need to say who we are and get it out of the way. I think they may be waiting for that.'

'Who are we?'

'I'll think of something.'

'I love you.'

'Yes, and so you should.'

The birthday party was extremely sticky to begin with. We had bought nibbles and little quiches from the gently sardonic wife of the man who ran a charcuterie in Beauvais. She was at a loss to say what people would expect of us and we blundered badly by offering wine when pastis might have been better. Gilbert and his glamorous wife stunned the neighbours, almost as much as the table improvised from a door. But the star of the show was the wise and imperturbable Dorothea Alcock, whose good nature ironed out the little local difficulty of getting close neighbours to talk to each other. Her French was as impeccable as her manners. Madame Pasquet sat silent, her lips twitching into a smile when someone gallantly complimented Liz on the skill she had shown with the baking of the quiche.

'You see this woolly stuff here at the foot of the wall?' John Alcock asked.

'Saltpetre,' Jean-Yves replied.

'Yes, but did you know that when Napoleon became First Consul, he sent teams of inspectors to find and harvest the stuff for the making of gunpowder?'

'Yes.'

'Oh, you did?'

John knew John le Carré, though under what circumstances he did not say. His first foreign language was German, though he too spoke impeccable French. He was disposed to indulge us as bumbling nobodies – goodhearted perhaps, but innocents abroad.

'Strictly speaking, this is an unimportant and badly constructed farmhouse. I hope you are good at what I think they still call in England do-it-yourself,' he told me. 'Do you have any tertiary education, by the way?'

'I read English at Cambridge.'

'Oh dear,' he chuckled. 'Not a very great preparation for life.'

Paulette Ayraud brought along her son and daughter-in-law together with Romain, but also her granddaughters, the bustily shy teenagers Melanie and Céline. They in turn were squired by their boyfriends, two hearty lads who looked around the ground floor with secret amusement. They all asked for Coca-Cola, which we had not thought to provide. Nor did we have enough receptacles to display the flowers brought as gifts. Under no compulsion to make what the English call small talk, the party broke up into groups of men discussing the maize harvest and what the distillers were saying about the outlook for the *vendange*. Their womenfolk bombarded Liz with recipes. The teenagers went into a huddle and composed thank-you poems before roaring off into the sunset on their mobilettes:

> *L'invitation a venir*
> *Illumine mon coeur.*
> *Soyaitez les bienvenus*
> *En notre demeuere.*

Madame Daniaud was the first to leave. Her old dad, who lived with her, had fought at Gallipoli and was coming up to his hundredth year. His collection of medals was displayed on velvet in a picture frame. Several knowledge-able experts had passed favourable comment. And at Nontron, where he had been born, he was still remembered with affection.

'He was a hairdresser,' her husband explained with a sly smile.

'And a soldier,' she added sharply. 'A true hero.'

'And, Jean,' I asked. 'Were you too a soldier once?'

'Yes,' Mme Daniaud answered for him. 'But hardly a hero. Hardly an Achilles.'

If John Alcock was dubious about our qualifications to call ourselves writers, she was not. She had already lent us devotional books – or at least, delivered them to the doorstep with a little card depicting Jesus walking in an olive grove.

The last of the neighbours to leave was Martine Ayraud.

'You have tried to be friendly with everybody as you promised,' she smiled. 'I congratulate you.'

'We made a number of mistakes.'

'You are too hard on yourself, madame. Arranging the flowers in Gaston's old buckets was a clever idea. Everybody knows you have yet to settle in. And tomorrow expect enough tomatoes and courgettes to feed a regiment. You'll see.'

And so we ended up with John and Dorothea Alcock and their granddaughter Kate, lit by candles, sitting on a travel rug and drinking wine in the English manner, which is to say with quiet determination.

'You will have discovered the ubiquity of the millepede,' he said.

'I have,' Kate said feelingly.

'They are perfectly harmless.'

'But proprietorial,' Liz suggested. 'We have one in the loo that seems a bit miffed at the way things are going.'

'Where on earth do they go at night?' Kate asked.

'Perhaps they are cleaning their boots?' I suggested.

'Some minor public school whimsy is at play, possibly.'

'John comes from Manchester originally. It's made him chippy,' his wife said cheerfully. 'And you,' she added, 'from one of the London boroughs, I think.'

'Lambeth. I was born in Lambeth Walk.'

'Cripes,' her granddaughter said. 'So that thing about the boots was an example of cockney humour.'

'Or an incurable facetiousness,' Liz murmured.

'Did you know that in the eighteenth century Lambeth was noted for its spa fields?' John asked.

'Yes.'

'Oh, you did?'

'Did you know that Jean-Pierre Ayraud, who was here tonight, can divine for water?'

'Are there hazels to be found here? It seems unlikely.'

'He uses a wire coat hanger.'

'Do you know what those double plums we ate tonight are called?' Dorothea asked her granddaughter. '*Les Couillons du Pape.*'

It was one in the morning before they left. John backed his car into the wall of the house, smashing both rear lights, and then missed the gatepost by millimetres.

'Life is such an adventure,' Dorothea said breezily, kissing her hostess goodnight.

A week or so later, Liz wrote to her daughter in Colorado. 'Our/my party was OK, I think: at least it announced our good will and was repaid fourfold: you only had to show your difficulty with, say, tiling or knocking down a wall or you-name-it and they'd burst in and help; plus give you the contents of their veg gardens, samples of their rillettes, pâtés, terrines . . . What a do it all was. Your true country person cannot be a solitary and if we spend more than just a month or so there in the future, I'm going to have to find somewhere to hide – e.g. under a bush – and there are none yet on our property . . .'

8

Paper Games and Moonlight

While looking for far more relevant things in Liz's desk, I came across this, written I think at the house in France one balmy evening in 1993. The poem is a composite of individually written couplets and the handwriting indicates that the order in which they were composed is Brian/Roger/Whiz.

> Colonel Weston threw his coat down,
> Then his regimental tie;
> Barked an order to his batman
> 'Unbutton, man, your C.O.'s fly!
> First salute, then kneel and look.
> Gently now – the man's an ass.'
> (The Colonel not a man to brook
> A servant that was crude or crass.)
> 'Good God, sir! Were you not aware
> That officers have willies too?'
> At which the willing trooper swore
> He'd never seen a finer view . . .

Roger was a perfect guest – shy, but with the capacity and appetite to be extremely skittish. He and his sister both loved paper games and the three of us spent many delirious evenings writing limericks, lewd Consequences and scandalous literary pastiches, while all around us the hamlet slept and the moon smirked over the maize fields.

He was a great map-reader. Whenever he drove to see us, he used a 1934 *Daily Mail Road Atlas* with the motorways and post-war trunk roads pencilled in. This was thrifty of him, but it also offered the opportunity to mourn the obliteration of some quite fascinating B-roads that had been sacrificed in the name of progress, an idea Roger deplored. He believed there was in England a great cloud of conspirators – vandals with pens and clipboards who built nuclear power stations and motorways wherever they fancied, poisoned the mind of the young with pop music, decimated the population of peewits and marsh warblers, and forced supermarkets to sell wholly unsuitable apples.

Whenever we planned a car excursion in France to somewhere we knew well, he would sit next to me with the local map on his knee.

'There is an alternative route which – oh, well, it doesn't matter, you've just passed the turning.' Then might follow a few moments of silent study and then: 'I calculate it is 1.4 kilometres shorter, that's if you ever want to try it.'

'Our way is quicker, Roger,' Liz would say.

'Oh, I don't doubt it. But you miss running along the little stream that' – more silence, more map rustling – 'yes, that comes out eventually at Massac. Which seems a pretty modest blot on the landscape.'

He was of course paying the place a compliment. That

summer we sat opposite each other in Gaston's yard, digging holes in the limestone in which to plant two trees we had yet to buy. Our tools were a cold chisel and a fireman's axe. Any fragment we dislodged at one blow that was bigger than a matchbox was reckoned a major victory. We soon agreed between us that a hole a cubic metre in size was about as much as we could manage. The trees must take their chance.

'It doesn't seem much of a chance from here,' Liz objected.

'From here it does,' her brother grunted, his vest stuck to his torso by sweat, his father's straw hat jammed on his head. It was ventilated by long horizontal rips held together by the merest wisps of Panamanian straw. If the Crazy Gang had ever felt the need for an Old Harrovian straight man, Roger would have walked into the part, unauditioned.

One evening Jean-Yves brought his wife and boys round to measure the depth of the well. Roger explained that this could be easily done by timing the fall of a rock down the shaft and listening for the splash made when it hit the water. The rest was elementary mathematics. The two young Boucherie boys exchanged glances.

'The first thing is not to stumble and fall down the well yourself,' Liz yelped. Jean-Yves held him safe by the waist-band of his jeans as the measurement was made.

'Twenty-five metres,' Roger confirmed.

'Michael, run and fetch me the thirty-metre measure.'

'Well, we shall see,' Roger said, but not without a dubious glance at the wristwatch he was holding in his hand. 'I didn't actually hear the splash myself but I trust you all to have called out —'

73

Michael returned with the tape measure. The well was eighteen metres deep.

'If you say so,' Roger muttered. With this same watch and navigating by dead reckoning, he had several times sailed to France across the English Channel, never missing a landfall.

Later that week, Liz insisted that we did something to prevent her grandchildren from falling down the well, no matter how deep or shallow it was. I hit on what I thought of as an elegant solution. I bought a section of sewage pipe a metre and a half across and the same in height. It was made of concrete five centimetres thick and delivered by a truck with a crane. The idea was to roll it into position and then (somehow) tip it upright.

'Everything will depend on the length of the fulcrum,' Roger observed from the bottom of the yard. 'Or rather, the lever that —'

The truck that brought it had hardly gone out of sight before I discovered that I could not move the pipe, let alone manouevre it into position.

Roger laid down his book of crossword puzzles and marched up the garden, the crown to his straw hat bouncing gently. This was just his kind of challenge. We might start, he suggested, with a few grains of sand in front of the pipe, gradually adding more. The ramp that resulted was the way the block stone of the pyramids had been raised. The problem was that we had no slaves at hand to help. Moreover, the path to the well was littered with rocky outcrops. This was for Roger a minor, almost an insignificant problem. How had Hannibal crossed the Alps, after all? We could pour vinegar – if not that, the kind of wine that came in plastic containers – over the rocks and so break them up.

'I think,' Liz said, 'the rocks have first to be heated. The image of white heat comes to mind from somewhere.'

'Well,' Roger conceded grumpily, 'that may be so. We shall need a line of bonfires, therefore – or yes! several bags of barbeque charcoal – and quite a lot of cheap wine.'

Just then, Jean-Yves made a sauntering visit in his green work overalls and had the scheme outlined to him. His silence on the subject was painful. It was the hour of day when the red sun was crashing down in the west. Overhead were the vapour trails of impossibly high planes, no larger than silver blips, each of them filled with passengers who had seldom, if ever, thought about Hannibal. They were suspended inside their own magic box of tricks, lit by the glories of the sunset and thinking about, if anything at all, deep-vein thrombosis.

Jean-Yves strolled back to his yard, fired up the tractor with the forklift attachments, came back with two nylon slings around his neck and in two minutes laid the concrete pipe over the well. But, being Jean-Yves, he had also brought along a three-metre spirit level. He raised the pipe an inch or so, chocked it up on one side, let it fall exactly *comme il faut*, which was to say dead centre and perfectly level, nodded politely to Liz and drove out of the yard. Roger was still smarting from the well-measuring debacle earlier in the week.

'Yes, he's good at the practice of the thing, I grant him that. But a bit weak on theory,' he commented sourly.

These days with Liz and her sibling were among the happiest I ever spent in France. In their company, I was looking back through the years to a time when two very intelligent children amused each other in the languor (as I imagined it) of an upper middle-class family not especially wedded to the written word. They shared a preference for solitary reflection, offset by a mutual love of music and general intellectual curiosity. Like Liz's son Thomas, Roger was the boy among three girls and the comparison led me to use their first names interchangeably. He never corrected me. His extreme aversion to being told what to do and think mirrored Thomas's. And like Thomas, his view of human nature was unforgiving.

'I have always thought the world would be a better place if human beings were absent from it altogether,' he said one night, slicing his daily apple.

'How would we know?'

'We wouldn't need to know.'

'No, but how could your assertion ever be tested?'

'Is that the point?' he asked, peering. 'Things got on very well without us for some tens of millions of years, I have always heard. Perhaps I am just indicating a preference.'

The subject cropped up in that night's batch of limericks.

> A dinosaur said to his mate
> 'I'm awfully sorry I'm late.'
> An anthropomorphic construct
> That's most seriously f*cked
> The whole point of our recent debate.

But then again, Roger, like Liz, had the best part of his mind concentrated elsewhere. He made music, working at a dogged pace with the utmost seriousness. And like Liz, he was at heart indifferent to what other people thought of what he was doing and hardly ever bothered to explain it. He understood his sister and admired her work – he asked her some very intelligent questions about how the novels could be interpreted – but his response to her was almost visceral. It was a sympathy she reciprocated. They were peas in a pod.

In 1981 Liz published *Dames*, a novel I have always considered her best. Dames is a school for the daughters of the upper middle class and into this book Liz poured all her wit and compassion, her understanding of love and the disappointments that follow from a woman's mere obedience. Technically her most ambitious novel, it is also her most complete and whole. The book you are reading now is a smudged sketch of what she was, of the inimitable voice she had. Her intellectual life was nurtured by the actual school on which Dames is modelled – not a difficult puzzle to solve – a place for which she retained a lifelong affection. She had stories of being posted back to it each term, a wan and hungry child with a cheap black suitcase, made dizzy by cigarettes she could not finish and tortured by chilblains. There were conversations with other travellers – vicars, countrywomen and, on one dangerous occasion, an exceedingly drunk sailor.

The feminism for which the school was famous – and which protected the girls from roguery in carriages without connecting corridors – underpins the story. The men in the book – the husbands and lovers – are sliced and diced like carrots. All that's required from the best of them – and they are very few in number – is that they are kind. Here's Phillida Hackstraw, in the last days of the mission that Dames has set up in Ethiopia. It is a place set aside to do good in the world but also to help Old Damians come to terms with life's disappointments. The unmarried and over-hearty Phillida is talking to her school contemporary Mousey, shortly before disaster overtakes them both.

'I do remember once,' said Phillida, 'the Founder sent me off one day as a punishment to count the pine trees in the bit of ground around Miss Dumont's hut. I had done something silly and I had to count these blooming pine trees . . .'

'A rather useless punishment?'

'The idea was that it *was* a useless punishment. She said we'd spend our lives, or half of them, doing useless things and so we might as well start now.'

'Perhaps she meant the ones who married . . . you know, washing, cooking.'

'They'd like us to think so, wouldn't they, the married ones? But that is balls, with due respect, Hilary. They love to talk about this coping they have to do and saying life is hectic, but if you can't cope with what men ask of you and do to you, you do deserve a useless punishment . . .'

Later, Mousey – the incomparable Mousey – lies in bed writing a letter she will never send to Ted, the kind man in her life who is also someone else's husband.

'I think that all I want is that some time somewhere, you look up from your work or eating a boiled egg or at a meal and make it known, if only by expression, that your mind is far away from those around you and you are not altogether theirs. That way I might exist again . . .'

The useless punishment they have been talking about is heading their way, heartless and implacable. It will arrive in the morning by jeep, in the form of two rebel soldiers with itchy trigger fingers.

One of the reasons we came to Oxford was to be close to Deb Gill, or as the Old Damians would have put it, Deborah (Spranger) Gill. Another Damian, Shirley (Du Boulay) Harriot lived only a few hundred yards away, in that part of North Oxford where the houses are immense and every home is crammed with good intentions and an unflinching belief in intellect. Deb was Liz's lifelong friend, rich (in my terms very rich), self-absorbed, beautiful and, in the spirit of Liz's novel, heroically disappointed by the way things turn out. *Dames* is dedicated to her and seldom has a dedication been more apt. Whenever we drove home across the water meadows, I always felt I was stealing Liz away from the world to which she most truly belonged.

'You mean the house? You'd have to have made it big as a potted meat magnate to live there.'

'I was thinking of all the awesomely intelligent and gifted people you could have known.'

'I have no answer to that,' she said drily. 'What do you say we stop at the Mediterranean for fish and chips?'

Shirley Harriot was our introduction to Oxford Writers, a loose collection of dry old sticks and green sappy ones. We were not the kind of writers likely to make a mark in this group, whose social evenings were replete with the best food and extremely good wines, accompanied by desultory conversation, not altogether about the sharper end of the business. I once asked a rather glamorous woman with an expensive cashmere shawl her name. She had been quizzing the room for half an hour with a faint half-smile on her lips.

'Well, I have eight writing names,' she replied calmly. 'Which one would you like to hear first?'

Liz was very good in such circumstances. There was a history to it. In 1964 she had driven into Bridport at Christmas time and bought herself a notebook in which she planned at first to write down *bons mots* and interesting topics for use at dinner parties. (Such occasions otherwise gave her migraine.) She assumed, very unwisely, that the sort of Dorset people who gave dinner parties were also cultured and highly intelligent. She needed to make notes of smart things to say. The example she gives in the first page or so is of interrupting a conversation over the chocolate mousse by inserting something she had cribbed from that day's edition of the radio programme, *The Critics*.

'Oh,' she cried, 'what a plastically intelligent comment on the affluent society!'

The men stared at her as though the devil had stolen her wits away. Their wives looked into their plates in pity.

When the dinners were given at her own house, her commonplace book subsides into more practical matters – 'the Vicar does not like prawns' is an example. There are glimpses of home life. 'Is it lower middle to require whites to be ultra white?' More dolefully, and perhaps arising directly from that particular question: 'A bad washing day is one where I keep getting my feet wet.' But she soon finds her stride and writes things down for their own sake: 'GPY's aunt: I just said No Bid all evening and no one knew that I couldn't play bridge'; 'If you stood her up sideways you'd mark her absent'; 'A young girl calls to her lover / when you see green smoke coming from our chimney / do not call at our house / for that will be the day we are burning wredlbitz / and that will be the day my mother is at home.'

The thing that comes out of this first notebook is the amount of borrowings she made from the Dorset Library Service's travelling vans. (They included *The Story of O*, for which we must hope she is still remembered by the young librarian who issued it). A more gnomic entry is this: 'Paleomon rode on a dolphin'. Was this research into Greek myth? And if so, was it sparked by the 1957 Negulesco film *Boy on a Dolphin* starring Alan Ladd and a young Sophia Loren? The movie doesn't seem her kind of entertainment at all, unless she was attracted to the gossip that in the scenes where Ladd and Loren sauntered romantically down a beach, she was obliged to walk in a trench to equalize their heights.

On the second page of the notebook is a much more revealing entry, a quotation from the liberal theologian, Richard Rumbold.

'Is any form of life worthwhile which does not strike into the deeper, more imaginative centres of one's mind and which does not make one aware constantly of its mystery? It doesn't much matter whether it is the life of a Trappist monk in love with God or of a creative writer, or a life of heroic action, or a life lived close to nature – so long as it has this imaginative and, yes, miraculous quality and so long as it nourishes the roots of one's being.'

Liz was thirty-two when she wrote this down and had been married for thirteen years. One of her children has lately described the marriage as a safe haven. By the time her mother went into Bridport and bought the notebook, however, she was a woman who realized that anything she was going to do in life, anything that embodied the spirit of Bishop Rumbold's exhortation, she was going to have to do alone. She was becoming an embarrassment to her husband, who was put to the trouble of explaining her away as the daughter of an eccentric mother, or commending her to others in a jocular sort of way, as one might a dog that could balance biscuits on the end of its nose.

After all, it was not expected that women should worry their pretty little heads about anything they heard at a dinner party. Their job was to cook well and keep the children out of the room, remember the more significant illnesses of other people's elderly relatives, heap praise where it was due for a show of delphiniums or a new summer house, decry the government and shake their heads over the ruination of colonial rule in Africa. All the rest was wallpaper and soft furnishings, sherry and sensible shoes. It was certainly not their way to quote Byron favourably and quite shocking that the wife of that rather nice man David Howard did. Whether Liz actually shared this snippet with them at dinner parties, she certainly made a note of it:

> There is a tide in the affairs of women
> Which, taken at the flood, leads God
> knows where . . .

Maybe before the ink dried she saw beyond the impudence. This was a simple description of how she was placed; and an invitation to break free.

At the very end of his life, David self-published his autobiography. In it he discusses briefly his reaction to his wife's first novel and the changes wrought in her by their move from Dorset to Yorkshire. She had, he felt, become political. It is a heart-rending way of putting it, for I think he wanted to indicate that somehow she had renounced all that he held important in life, which was belonging to the right social class. He could recognise himself in the book but not, it seems, her. More narrowly, he fails to ask himself what made her want to write about married couples in such an acerbic way. He consults with authors and publishers of his acquaintance, as he puts it, as to whether she's any good, much as a man might seek a medical opinion about his wife's nervous condition. When the final break comes, it is, he claims, a complete surprise. He is told about his wife's adultery at the fag-end of yet another dinner party. Good manners, of the kind that he had cultivated so assiduously, forbade him from mentioning to his host his own numerous delinquencies in this area.

9

Some Deaths

In England, there was an elephant in the room – the fate of my parents. They ended up their lives banging about in a 1930s bungalow in Hertford that, had they been anyone else, would have been a triumph of managed retirement. My father's pension from the Post Office Engineering Branch was generous and from it he maintained four separate building society accounts – financial secrets kept inside a veneer and matchwood escritoire which for me merely to walk past was cause for suspicion. But age and infirmity had somehow uncoupled him from the lie he had lived and returned him to the Lambeth working class he so much despised. His business suits and several dozen ties and cravats, scarves and yellow cardigans were eaten by moths. The close-shaved cheeks that had once distinguished him among his fellow-commuters were gone, too. Old age and a lifetime of disdain had coarsened him. Now it was not just his family that was contemptible but the whole world. He shambled about the last years of his life like a wild man from the woods. Visiting him in this state was unbearable.

My mother meanwhile was sinking into dementia, stoked by an habitual (and incurable) anxiety that all that she had would be confiscated. She was of course terrified by doctors, who had nothing to offer except punishment and incarceration. Her life had come full circle. She answered the door to no one and if the phone rang, refused to answer. The garden was out of bounds because if she was seen there kindly neighbours would ask her how she was. They were spies, reporting back to some shadowy Ministry.

'I don't think we've ever had a kind word out of her,' a neighbour complained. 'And, really, her language is just terrible. She called my husband a poxed-up four-eyed know-nothing git. He is a college lecturer.'

A guileless GP had prescribed her the sedative Mandrax and my father went every so often to get her a repeat prescription. The airing cupboard contained enough unopened boxes of this drug to poison the entire street. When I went to the surgery to complain, I discovered that the doctor who had first given her this medicine had been dead five years. His successor had visited the house once and found no reply to his knock. Peering on tiptoe over the back gate, he saw a dishevelled figure he took to be a jobbing gardener waving him away with a spade, up to his hips in grass and weeds. Inside the bungalow, Radio 1 was playing, loud enough to strip the wallpaper. Busy man, he shrugged his shoulders and left.

In time there were emergency ambulances and hospital admissions, clinical assessments and day care appointments that neither of them kept. When he had a stroke, she left him untended on the bedroom floor for three days before a next-door neighbour's wife discovered him. My mother ran down the road after the ambulance, shouting that she could not and would not pay them. When it was her turn to fall out of bed and break her cheekbone and wrist, the nurses at the cottage hospital told me in wondering tones they had found £800 in her handbag. Rotten son that I was, I failed to ask for a receipt. The money disappeared. Looking at it another way, it went to where it could do some good.

I sustained them in their own home for as long as I could, looked after twice a day by a fearless gay carer called Malcolm, who played them his Judy Garland faves and propped them up, this way and that. The only thing he found alarming was the number of cigarettes they smoked.

'It's a wonder they haven't burned the house down,' he said. 'The air in there is blue. Dad thinks he's still in charge of things, of course, but your mum is very low. And the carpets! You really don't want to know about the carpets. It's lovely, what you are trying to do for them but it can't go on. It must be killing you, driving down from Yorkshire every week.'

'It's what they want. To live in their own home.'

'You must be very soft-headed, to let them have what they want. And you never told me your father was the holder of a Victoria Cross, by the way.'

'You must have guessed that isn't true, Malcolm.'

'About those two, nothing would surprise me. I sometimes go home and talk to Derek about them all night.'

Malcolm believed in the cleaning products he'd seen advertised on television – especially those delivered from an aerosol can. Though he bombed the place with lavender and pine, alpine meadow and all the rest of it, he could not mask an awful faecal stink. Outside, what had once been my father's pride and joy, a garden worthy of his ambitions, was now no more than a meadow. His scratch-built greenhouse leaned like a drunk against a lamp-post, held from falling by the plum tree he had tried for years to coax into fruit.

After eight months, I moved them into a nursing home. This is too brief a way of describing what happened. My father was hospitalised after a second mild stroke and wandered about, both blocking a bed and disrupting the management of the ward. He had the impression he was on the fifth floor and several times pointed out to me the statue of Air Marshal Lord Tedder in the grounds. His ward was in fact in a single-storey building and what we were looking at was a mossy gnome with a pointy hat and red shoes. I arranged that he should be discharged and driven by ambulance directly to the nursing home I had chosen for them both. I went back to the house and talked to my mother for twelve hours before she reluctantly agreed to join him. The threat – and it was not a very compelling one – was that if she did not, she would never see me again.

'We've got no money to spend on your poncy schemes,' she mumbled.

But I had looked inside the fabled escritoire and found that they were rich, richer than they had ever imagined possible in the Lambeth days. For forty years my mother had bought all her clothes at jumble sales, including shoes. He liked to buy the best for himself but she took that to be his prerogative. He was, in the end, the man of the house. Nor could she rid herself of the idea that he was also her jailer.

'One word from him and I'm back in the nuthouse.'

'That's not going to happen. He's old and feeble. I'm doing this for your sake, Mum. You get looked after, the place is warm, there's a garden —'

'What do I need with a fucking garden?' she bellowed, with the last of her manic energy. Two days later, she joined him in the nursing home.

To my amazement, she died first, for I had always thought of her, despite all the veils she lived behind – or perhaps because of them – as being the more wily and resilient. But during my last visits her eyes had lost all their colour and her expression was settled into haggard indifference. The two of them sat on opposite sides of the residents' lounge, whiling away the empty hours. Even their mutual hatred had ended. My father lived on for another year without her, having promoted himself to being the Chief Constable of Europe. The Assistant Matron believed in the VC but jibbed at all the rest.

'My husband's a police officer,' she warned darkly. 'They take a dim view of that sort of thing.'

'He has forgotten who I am,' I said.

'He doesn't want to remember, that's all.'

'Has he ever mentioned my mother since she died?'

'He's not that kind of person.'

I am editing their last two years because so much of it was squalid beyond words. When he died, my lifelong quarrel with him ended – like an archive closing, being bound with red tape and then filed away in some dusty warehouse out along the ring road. I rang my brother in Australia and offered to pay his fare to the funeral. His laconic reply summed up the utter dysfunction we had experienced as a family.

'That's good of you, mate, but I've just had a fortnight's holiday.'

'I'm not talking about a holiday, for God's sake.'

'No worries, Bri. That's all a long time ago, all that stuff. If there's any money coming, we can divvy that up when you're ready.'

Back at the house, I gave away the new fridge and washing machine I had bought them and took the rest – everything, down to the washing-up bowl – to the tip. Someone came from Bristol to drive away his car. In one day, a whole history was destroyed, leaving only the stain of its existence. Fewer than fifteen people attended each of the two funerals. And now, today, I cannot remember the month or year in which each of them died.

From time to time my mother has appeared to me in dreams, a sardonic slattern leaning against the door frame, or sitting smoking at the dining-room table, her head in her hands. But she has visited less and less often. As to my father, he entered eternity without a backward glance.

I am saying all this, because it contrasts so completely with Liz's own experience of family – or rather to say, with what she gave her children to remember and cherish her by. Her genius was to let them be who they wanted to be at whatever secret cost to herself. In return, they gave her unconditional love. Someone said at her funeral that she died without an enemy in the world. That suggests a saintly character I do not think she possessed. To live without enemies was a calculation she made in favour of a quiet life.

'People are who they are,' she explained to me over

and over. 'It's not your fault that you want to improve them. But, really, there's not much point in trying.'

The whole impulse for the writing of *Keeping Mum*, which is how the first volume of this autobiography begins, was to set down who we were when I was a child, in the hope that my grandchildren and their children might know something of the past. I hoped the smartest among them might also find in the book an explanation (though not a justification) of who I became as a man.

'You are a complete mess,' Liz confirmed. 'People see you as a very difficult and insecure person. But I like you and need you. And, of course, you like me, which will always weigh heavily in your favour.'

'I tried —'

'Yes, I know you did. Your parents were undone by the march of time. Nothing and no one could have saved them. It happens everywhere. It will happen to us.'

'Not to you.'

'Of course to me. To everyone.'

When her own mother died, it was – at least on the surface – a more dignified departure. Eilean's funeral service was conducted by a foolish sort of vicar in a church that he had ruined by having the pews rearranged to resemble theatre in the round. His evocation of her life and personality was a vulgar approximation of who she actually was, and what goodness she had in her heart. Her accent and the title that went with it invited gentle guying and much of what he had to say was meant to amuse. Things, he seem to imply, had moved on since her day. And this was undoubtedly true. She had no say in the populism he wished to encourage among his parishioners and I think the one thing she could do without in her life was jolliness. She might have said of her own funeral that parts of it were extremely tiresome. She was not, as he caricatured her, some upper-class old fossil who followed him (as she did) out of respect for his gospel, difficult as it was for her to understand this way of pouring new wine into old bottles. He happened to be vicar of the parish church and you took what you were given.

During the commital service, I noticed that he was wearing shoes without socks. He had recently been in India and came home with a thing about socks and electric kettles, labour-saving devices and the like. It occurred to me that women like Eilean North believed they had a duty to conceal their true feelings. To do anything else would be bad form. It is the antithesis of the rowdy and incoherent life my own mother had lived. I knew all about that – the spiteful and half-maddened hectoring, the need to retaliate before the first blow had been struck, the sheer carelessness of speech and conduct that ensued. Recklessness had dogged my own life and spoiled me as a person. I was my mother's child. But watching the vicar slide about at the edge of the grave in his sockless shoes filled me with rage and pity. We were saying goodbye to a lonely and disappointed woman, to be sure, but one who every night could be found at prayer. Eilean was devout beyond the vicar's understanding.

We moved to Oxford, where this is being written. And not to Colin Dexter's version of Oxford either but a leafy-laned suburb within level walking distance of three hospitals, three supermarkets and two chippies. The spaces in between were taken up by charity shops. It was hard to ignore the hospitals, for the day was punctuated by the howl of police and ambulance sirens and at night emergency helicopters hovered low overhead. I never associated any of this with death and disaster. It was somebody else's story.

I had come almost to the end of writing for television. A new kind of sensibility was at work – earnest, po-faced and above all, populist in temper. Almost the last thing I ever wrote in this medium was an episode or so for a series set in wartime. The originating author was a gloomy woman about my children's age.

'Mmm,' she said. 'I gave you an episode to write in which Ralph and Tom have homosexual feelings for each other. But I think that's probably wrong and we ought to change the storyline.'

'A bit too obvious, do you think, even for this load of nonsense?'

She studied me with neutral green eyes. 'What I'm saying is that I'm not sure there was any homosexuality in the 1940s.'

'Good point. I've read somewhere that it was invented at Keele University in the late seventies. Let's run with that. And, of course, can we even be sure that the Germans won the war?'

From conversations like these there was no way back. I sent a script to Alan Ayckbourn, who had directed three of my earlier stage plays. After eight weeks I got back a gentle postcard which read in its entirety 'So that's where you are!'. He trusted me to draw my own conclusions. The play's subject was the haunting of my house by my parents and not even the great play-doctor George Kaufman could have saved it.

Liz had also written her last novel. What we knew

about fiction we taught at Oxford's Department of Continuing Education, our course buttressed by some very scholarly but recondite competitors. We represented the sprawling talents of students who wanted to be published first and foremost and whose adherence to theory and the notion of 'literature' was comfortingly sketchy. The classes were huge in comparison to the general level of enrolment and intensely practical in method. They were workshops. The presumption was that everyone who stayed the course would end up with the first draft of a long work of fiction.

I should add that since the popularity of so-called reading groups, courses like ours are, I think, harder to find, certainly at the level of extra-mural teaching. What is sometimes called 'the serious novel' has skewed the teaching of literature, so that (again, in my experience) reading has become more of a devotional exercise, much as it was in the nineteenth century. It is rare to find among reading groups any enthusiasm for work outside the canon. In this way John le Carré and Patrick O'Brian are seldom discussed with any seriousness, any more than the work of possibly one of our greatest contemporary English moralists, Alan Ayckbourn.

Liz had twice been a writer-in-residence, twice more a writer-in-schools and had taught at both Arvon sites. She had a genius for this kind of work – patient, encouraging, provoking when needs be, but always on the side of rigorous honesty. In short, she encouraged virtue. Her reputation grew, to the point where students she had never met and would never meet face to face appeared on the doormat as if from nowhere, submitting their book-length manuscripts and asking for advice and commentary.

'I have now gathered all your wonderful novels onto

my shelves. I could never write as well as that,' an admirer gushed.

'Neither can I any longer,' she replied by postcard, thought the better of sending it and shoved it down a notorious gap between the fireplace and the wall, where it rests today.

'Damn,' she said bleakly.

I went back to France twice that winter, the first time with my son Steve and a long-time friend, Pete Thomson. His witty and glamorous wife Ann had provided a shoebox with things not certain to be found across the Channel – like sweeties and fresh fruit but also two rolls of toilet paper. We worked in CEGB coveralls in miserably frosty conditions with the sort of materials suitable for do-it-yourself renovation of a semi-detached lounge in Leeds or setting a suburban garage roof to rights. Our neighbour Jean-Yves found our efforts pitiful. What we needed, he explained, was to build at least one false interior wall supported on metal framing. We sent for details and received by return of post an explanatory video in which a young man and his smiley wife performed the erection without a single hitch. It was all so simple.

Pete and I had once built a Mirror dinghy with the same naïve trust, spurred on by publicity materials explaining that a group of Girl Guides had run up their dinghy in less than a day. It took us a couple of months and when we put the boat in the water it leaked in four places. As for the present work in hand, Jean-Yves, who expected very little from British workmen, had his worst doubts confirmed. We floundered. Every element of the false wall design defeated us. It was pointless to say in our defence that we were bringing to the job the ill-assorted talents of a writer, jazz musician and an engineer who spent his time inspecting and repairing welds in nuclear power plants.

Jean-Yves was the antithesis of someone like Pierre Milhat. He was grave and formal to a fault but with a terrier-like persistence and a barnful of tools that would not have disgraced the centre isles of B&Q to go with it. He could measure, saw and cut, weld, braze and rivet: there was not a thing he could not do. The world of material objects, which so intimidated me, was his playground. I think he found us entertainingly pitiable; his own greatest pleasure was working with his hands. Over years to come, his interpretation of what we were trying to do with the place led to some spectacular acts of kindness, involving many hours of dedicated graft. It was hard at first to see why.

'You call me by my first name, which is acceptable, but I notice you address my wife always as madame. From this I see you are courteous and respectful, qualities not always apparent among the English.'

He really did speak in this orotund manner and there was nothing he liked more at the end of the day than foretelling the collapse of all manners and niceties among the French, the precursor, he thought, of revolution and bloody civil war. He held out little hope for the future.

'The rich have made themselves so by ignoring the lessons the poor learned at their mother's knee. One day soon society will go pouf,' he explained, clapping his hands to show how violent the sundering would be. 'Things cannot last as they are.'

His own mother's knee was capacious enough. Arlette

Boucherie was an old-time Frenchwoman with a passion for cooking and preserving things. We were invited to a meal. Pete was entranced, though he asked me to explain that in England we did not eat garlic because it made your breath smell. It was the garlic that did for him. For three days, this most mild-mannered of men lay in his bedroom at the Hôtel du Commerce, wrestling with his guts and cursing French cuisine up hill and down dale.

'Why put stuff in food they know is going to poison you?'

'She gave the green beans a particular thrashing,' my son Steve admitted. 'But look at it this way: have you seen a vampire come anywhere near us? I think they know more about that sort of thing than they're letting on. The custard pie at the end was nobby, though.'

He had eaten two helpings of what Liz later described as Arlette's Killer Flan. I mentioned to the company Jean-Yves' theories of the imminent collapse of Western civilisation.

'You can't miss what you never had,' his father chortled.

At which everyone in the room laughed uproariously. The story of the false wall had preceded us. The young Madame Boucherie – Ghislaine – caught my eye and smiled briefly.

'Perhaps *m'sieu* will tell us a little of what he is writing at the moment,' she suggested politely.

'A play about Marco Polo in prison, madame.'

'It sounds an important work.'

'I have to say, it throws very little light on such things as Gaston's house, your husband's kindness or the excellence of the food we have just eaten. I raise my glass to the cook.'

Arlette beamed and shovelled a second slice of the killer flan onto my empty plate.

I went back a second time in April of the following year with Stephen and his fellow guitarist, Piers. It was just as cold and the fires we attempted to light in the huge hearth filled the ground floor with roiling smoke. During the short hours of daylight we manoeuvred eight by four sheets of plasterboard, sliding about on the special fixative, sealing the joints with hessian scrim. Jean-Yves stuck his head around the door from time to time, bellowing instructions. There is a useful French word that should have, but did not, come into play – *finition*. It was all very well slamming the plasterboard into position but the end of all this labour was to make the joints invisible. Piers was excellent at measuring but Steve and I not so good at jointing. Jean-Yves' wall, with its metal frames, was just as good – and actually rather better than – the construction video that came with the kit. The three remaining walls had a bruised look even before the plaster had dried.

'We have to tell him we were going for just that effect,' Steve suggested. 'You know, insouciance.'

'Or whimsy.'

'Exactly. His wall is the Café de Paris, ours more of a Fats Waller thing.'

'*The Joint is Jumpin'*,' Piers suggested doubtfully.

Paul and Callie had taken Milhat at his word and brought over half a dozen string players to give concerts. They were sixth-formers whose lives up until now had been what Larkin calls, in a stark phrase, reprehensively perfect. They sat on the icy floor tiles in overcoats and scarves and listened to my two building labourers rip up some classic jazz standards, looking bewildered and uneasy. Guitars were for strummers. Three chords were plenty.

'How'd you learn to play like that?' one of them asked.

'Love comes into it,' Piers replied gravely. 'And hunger.'

The year 1993 was the tipping point. We had a *salle de séjour*, the beginnings of a kitchen, a wonderful pine staircase to the atelier, new doors and windows. During the winter M. Dieumegard had demolished the cow byre and two of the three barns. Jean-Yves had found a way of resiting the run-off and stench pipe of the *fosse d'étanche*, settling his improvements in Gaston's vegetable cellar in a far corner of the yard. Into this space, which had once cost God knew how many man-hours to cut from the limestone reef on which the property stood, we threw all the loose boulders, tiles and chunks of concrete that littered the yard. Before we left that spring, I commissioned two middle-aged brothers to put up the remaining plasterboard in what was now the kitchen and then go on to point the walls of the *grenier*. They were the kind of Frenchmen sent from heaven – massive, laconic and unjudgemental. When I mentioned the plasterboard to be fitted in the kitchen, they merely glanced and nodded, as if I had asked for nothing more challenging than hanging a picture, or squashing a wasp.

'Shall I pay you half in advance?' I asked. They found this amusing.

'Half in advance and we shall undoubtedly leave our wives and go down to the Côte d'Azur for the winter, *m'sieu.*'

10

Inconsolable

In November 1993 I went back out to France with Sophie, Liz's second daughter, to collect and plant the trees chosen to give greenery and shade for her mother in the following year. They were to go into the holes Roger and I had dug. It was a lesson in the dangers of wishful thinking. Mild enough when we set off, the further south we went, the colder the weather became.

The worst part of any visit to France was the six-hour journey from the Channel ports. I had learned to drive by teaching myself on regimental LandRovers in Kenya, two of which I overturned. I failed my first test in England, driving my father's 1930s Wolseley Hornet, which he bought from a neighbour for £70. It worked best when one or two clothes-pegs were employed to jam the choke open and the brass lever to the advance/retard ignition was set just right. The examiner studied these arrangements without comment. It was raining cats and dogs when we set off and when he tried to open the window a touch, the winder came off in his hand. Feeling spiteful, he pulled the clothes-pegs from the choke spindle. We stalled halfway round a roundabout.

'I take it the test is not going well.'

The examiner had a narrow skull and long neck. If he had ever smiled it was something he regretted.

'You can so take it,' he said in one of those choked, high-pitched voices from which some character actors have made a living.

This fiasco and a too close reading of the film *Wages of Fear* made me a cautious driver. After three hours on the autoroute, Sophie took over. She had learned to drive by jazzing around West London in a Royal Mail van. Our speed increased markedly, as did the cold.

We pitched up at Breuil in ten degrees of frost. It was one in the morning and we woke Jean-Yves' dogs into barking frenzy. Inside the house, tools were red with rust, an oil painting of a reclining nude had grown woolly grey underwear. Paperbacks had turned to frozen pulp. We lit a fire and the *salle de séjour* immediately filled with acrid blue smoke. It was – or it seemed – warmer outside than it was indoors. I don't know how she slept but I went to bed fully clothed with a plastic bin liner worn as a tabard. It was not enough.

In the morning it was quite clear that planting anything was out of the question. The sun had that pale metallic sheen that only happens in winter. The air was still but biting cold. All but one of the barns had been taken down, along with the cow byre, leaving jagged walls and mounds of stone and rubble. It was not a time for romantic reacquaintance with the beauties of France. I remember showing Sophie the holes we had dug in such sweltering heat and seeing her frown, for in winter light they looked ridiculously small and insignificant. They looked accidental, even.

Fortunately, she had brought her sketchbook with her and over the next couple of days donated pencil portraits of Mme Daniaud's father, the Gallipoli veteran, and Céline, Paulette Ayraud's granddaughter, in return for warmth and a kind word. For the neighbours, Sophie was easily the most understandable of Liz's children, having a native gift that corresponded to the practical skills they held dear. Anyone could be a doctor's wife and Thomas had queered his pitch among them by trying to reinvent Fernet Branca and offer it as an aperitif – he was later to poison himself for a few eventful days with a salad derived from weeds to be found in the garden. Rene Boucherie asked to be shown them.

'These kill cattle,' he explained bluntly.

As for Sophie, none of the communards of Breuil had ever been to an art gallery but they recognised worth when they saw it. It helped that she was extremely good-looking and very positive in outlook, something she had perhaps acquired in dramatic near misses along the Goldhawk Road. Earlier in the autumn, one of Elizabeth's students had limped into Breuil with an ailing Jaguar. Jean-Yves and one or two trusted friends spent three days taking the engine to pieces and then reassembling it. Sophie's sketches were out of the same box as the Jaguar engine block. They were worth taking the trouble to understand and repaid study with quiet pleasure.

Rural France when the sun has gone and days are short is no place to be. The summer calendar of roadside attractions and swimming holes, *frites* vans and melon stalls vanish; and with it the languor that makes the back country of France so appealing when it is hot. Now, even the lights of the great supermarkets seemed buttery yellow and unwelcoming. The car parks were filled with crusty and unwashed cars and the shoppers were bundled up like Ukrainian peasants. It was clear that without central heating and a sizeable stove, Liz and I could never winter over, not that she had ever contemplated that. After four days of shivering exploration, we beat an ignominious retreat.

While we were away, Liz had been in Bristol, looking after Sophie's son, who was three or four years old. When we got back, we found that he had been screaming and sobbing for his mother from the moment she left, breaking off only to kick and pummell his grandmother's legs in rage and exasperation. Now it was night and he was weak to the point of collapse. Liz was in the corner of the room, white-faced and exhausted. I had never seen such an expression on her face before. Something, some faceless snout pressed against the window pane, had come to torment her.

Over the next week, the pain took shape. It hurt that she could no longer soothe and pacify a child of her own blood. What she had to give was not enough. The food she cooked was thrown at her, her attempts to read aloud or sing produced even greater howls of rage. Though she tried to make light of these episodes to Sophie, she took the force of them home with her. When I explained that Rene Boucherie would plant the trees as soon as the weather broke, that children did cry for their mother and Sophie was not the kind to blame her for what had happened, she simply shrugged. She was inconsolable.

I did not know it then, but at this very same time she

was writing and making notes about her own mother. One of Eilean's favourite opinions was that, whatever the present shortcomings of children and grandchildren, there was, so to speak, plenty of time for the boat to right itself and rejoin the fleet. In her world, nobody ever came to grief completely, in part because they never sailed out of the sight of land. Meanwhile, it was better there was not a harsh word to be spoken about the family, down to its least member. This was the way she diffused any criticism that might otherwise be levelled at her. It was also a cultural imperative. Women of her era and class did not ask questions of themselves or their children – no good could come of it. She lived by a certain code, one that carefully excluded what E. M. Forster described as 'the outer world of telegrams and anger'. In these matters, time stood still. For example, there was no question that her husband had been cruelly sacrificed by Churchill in 1940. If she had an opinion about that, she kept it to herself. On the other hand, it was a matter of pride to know where everyone was and what they were doing. This led on occasions to surreal commentary on people I had never met.

'I believe he is a drug dealer in Amsterdam at the moment. But then he's always been interested in drugs and so I imagine he's doing it terribly, terribly well.'

On the face of it, Liz's mother was easy enough to understand. She was a product of her class, just as my mother had been. She was in her forties before she learned to cook something so simple as a boiled egg. We had in the house a blob of aluminium that had once been an empty saucepan. When she had let it heat on the gas stove to an incredible temperature, she saved the kitchen by opening the window and hurling the pan into a water butt. All that was left from the molecular explosion was this massy teardrop, small enough to hold in the palm of a hand.

She knew far more about Test cricket scores than the lives of the people who came to watch it. Her genuine gifts as a County Commissioner for Brownies stemmed largely from the innocence of her world view. Everything would be fine if only children learned not to be tiresome, or could rise above the penalty of having been born to tiresome parents. Signs that read 'TRESPASSERS WILL BE PROSECUTED' were doubtless necessary to deter others – say, people from the towns – but did not apply to her, as the landowners in question would surely agree. She would hoick up her skirt and lead her anxious grandchildren over the boundary wall. Black men and women did so well at the Olympics because they were used to running away from lions or hunting gazelles with spears. Some working-class people were awfully comical in speech and character but the best of them gave a wholehearted day's work for a day's pay. At National Trust properties she would step into the borders and break off sprigs of plants she felt would do well in her own garden. That rather nice man Percy Thrower had shown her on television how to strike these cuttings.

In 1936, she had gone to Bassano's in Dover Street to sit for a portrait photograph, still to be found in the National Portrait Gallery. The image shows a tall and rangy woman, with a long, unsmiling face, posed seated, and dressed in what look like country clothes. At the time of the photograph, Dudley North was commander of the royal yacht and the keeper of many bedroom secrets surrounding the Prince of Wales's royal tours and his association with Wallis Simpson. He was yet to be knighted (that happened the following year) but he was a senior naval officer with some of the acquired attributes of a royal courtier. There is no trace of any of this background in the expression on Eilean's face, which is carefully neutral. Whoever she was – whatever she was thinking when the photograph was taken – is absent from the pose she struck. Least of all can one imagine that this was a woman with four children.

Worldly Goods, Liz's 1987 novel, took as its plot the wedding of Nina Forestier to Campbell Crosby. It is not hard to assign real identities to these characters, who marry in the 1950s and are destined to repent at leisure. Eilean-as-Julia is also perfectly recognisable. Campbell comes from Yorkshire and she feels she must commend the county in some way. 'You have such lovely roses up there, don't you?' she gushes. 'It's the soot from the mines.' She is (to the general reader) a grand comic figure who irritates her daughter and astonishes the Crosbys but her presence is generally harmless. She does not escape Liz's sardonic attentions but she is by no means the engine of the book.

It was my habit never to ask detailed questions of Liz about her work, out of respect for her need for solitary contemplation. Nor did she volunteer information about what she was working on.

('What is it like to have two writers in the same house?' someone asked me once.

'About as exciting as having two traffic wardens'.)

We met in the evening for supper and gossiped for a couple of hours, before she excused herself and went back upstairs. Only since she's died have I seen what she was pondering at the time she babysat for Sophie. It was a sequel to *Worldly Goods*.

It seems an odd time to be going over old ground. By now Eilean was in her grave and the divorce from David twenty years (and two subsequent marriages) in the past. In this sequel, we discover that Nina has been unsatisfactorily married to Campbell for twelve years, which would have placed the action in real time back in Dorset, at the very moment when Liz was emancipating herself from what she regarded as the general nullity of upper middle-class life. But the story is thrown forward to Yorkshire and takes place 'in a barrack of a mansion which represented for her [Nina] all that was bleak and Brontë-ish about the north of England'. The skies have also darkened for Eilean–Julia. In the following extract she comes home to the house when it is momentarily empty.

Relieved that no one was in, she went to lie down on the spare room bed. And separated herself by sleep from all the problems that arose from sharing for a time in someone else's life. She rather wished she were at home again. Perhaps she hadn't done that well with Nina; but it hadn't felt she'd done all that badly at the time. Her daughter was, in fact, unknown to her, but no reason why that should worry her. That's how things are, she told herself, and her only other thought as she went into a doze was that she had no idea most of the time, what, in a broader sense, was happening . . .

Earlier in the day, greatly to Nina's anguish, she had been discussing her grandchildren with a visitor.

'Surely we should be talking about something more interesting than what my children are like,' thought Nina. 'Surely I should have the guts to override my mother's monologue . . .' This lead her to a bitter fit of self-examination. How banal her thoughts! How the trivia of life preoccupied her. How, when at last she had begun to think that she might become a thinking person with a few things worth saying . . . the opposite turns out to be the case!

These extracts from an unpublished draft can be dated so exactly because they are typed on the reverse of scrap paper – dated letters, play scripts of mine and the like. They are a long way from Colonel Weston and his desires and make uncomfortable reading for a very obvious reason. By that date, Liz had demonstrated beyond all doubt that she was a thinking person with a few things worth saying. The reviews of all eight novels were uniformly enthusiastic: she had additionally established herself as a tutor of exceptional merit. She had many friends – fellow novelists, poets, painters, musicians, broadcasters, academics. So much had changed in her personal life that she was unrecognisable from the Nina of *Worldly Goods*. It seems such a strange thing to me that she should want to revisit former stamping grounds, or feel so unchangingly bitter towards people she had already dealt with.

I would not be human if I did not feel guilty about this. I thought I knew her better than anyone else on earth, without the first idea of what it was that preoccupied her in these solitary stints upstairs. The projected novel was never completed but continued in one form or another until she died. At her funeral, someone remarked,

'I suppose most of the people here are your friends.' It seemed at the time a clumsy and ignorant remark but, in moments of despair, as now, seems more like an expertly driven stiletto between the ribs. Perhaps she never was mine in the way I supposed.

Dorset is the key. There was a timid and irresolute side to Liz that sprang from those early days. Nina is its incarnation. But then Nina never was Liz – perhaps better to say the woman I knew, or thought I knew. She had the gifts and the opportunity to overcome the things that oppressed her and certainly in general conversation she could not have been more dismissive of what she had left behind. But Dorset never really let her go. Towards the end of her life we spent a week there, driving about to places she remembered from childhood, she greatly vexed that so much had changed. Villages that once had schools and post offices, general stores and chapels even, had been gutted for the benefit of middle-class colonisers who had no need of any of these things. The Old School House was a merely a good address in these primped and remodelled communities. Pubs had become gastropubs, which was to say cute but quaint restaurants for the folk who find beer-drinking faintly vulgar. Wine lists had replaced the horse brasses.

After her death, one of her family, practising a newly acquired malice, said that she did no more than tolerate this kind of talk and that what made me so objectionable to others was shared by her, though she was too kind – or perhaps too politic – to make it an issue. I have thought about this. If it is true, then the whole of our time together was a self-deception.

'You are the one thing she can trust,' a friend contradicted.

'It seems a funny thing to be telling me in present circumstances.'

'This? This is just an overheated hotel room, two empty wine bottles and a rumpled bed. And some madwoman hoovering outside in the corridor at five in the afternoon. You are just someone thinking about catching a coach outside and going home.'

'Is that all it is?'

'She's not daft, she can easily imagine this happening, with me or someone else. It's another form of conversation, if you like.'

'A bit more than that, perhaps.'

'No. It's just an afternoon conversation. She loves you, you know that. But she thinks – I don't know, maybe she thinks – that telling you too often would spoil you.'

'She never tells me.'

'There you are then. Don't be needy. Tell me something. Will you stay with her right to the very end?'

'Of course.'

'Good. She's banking on it.'

We went back to France the following spring and found we had been invited to attend the annual dinner of the *Troisième Age*, a seven-plate bonanza that began at one in the afternoon and continued until six. One of the striking things about Charente Maritime is the longevity of its sons and daughters, as a glance at the obituary columns of *Le Sud-Ouest* can testify. Nor, it seems, do many of these senior citizens die in hospitals or old folks' homes. So it was in our commune. Some very ancient communards had turned out for the event. As happens in France, each course was appraised by beady-eyed experts.

'Whose soup is this?'

'Madame Gossuet's.'

'I thought so.'

'She herself is disappointed by it.'

'With good reason.'

I talked with an old man who had been captured by the Germans in the Second World War and sent to work on a farm near Münster. The farmer's daughter took a shine to him and all went well, until the girl's mother discovered them naked together in a barn.

'After that, I slept in a proper bed,' he said slyly.

'And where was the farmer?'

'Wehrmacht,' he answered, sketching a Hitler salute.

'Did you ever try to escape?'

He reached over and patted my hand gently.

'*Entre les deux, j'etais bien occupé, m'sieu.*'

'But you were glad all the same to get home.'

'*Pas tellement*,' a tiny old crone butted in with a seraphic smile. She was of course his wife.

As the afternoon wore on, there was singing, partly occasioned by the vagaries of the kitchen ovens, which blew the main fuses every ten minutes. Comic songs in the Charentais dialect were very popular, accompanied by expressive sexual gestures that set the table in a roar. We were asked to contribute and gave them '*Douce France*'. Trenet had been the poet-vagabond of this generation (incredibly, he was still alive and still touring) and we could not have chosen more wisely. Much did they care whether he collaborated during the war: he was the quintessential Frenchman in their eyes. The film star and *chanteuse* Arletty, who was actually imprisoned for collaboration, was likewise their idea of glamour. She was famous for a remark that, had she been a Charentaise, would have seen her stoned in the streets. Her crime was having slept with a German officer. She replied to the tribunal judging her: 'I may be a Frenchwoman from Courbevoie but my arse is international.' It was what Paris was for, that kind of laconic impudence. That it no longer existed was beside the point. For one glorious afternoon, in the most unlikely of all places, it lived again.

We came away as a frail old man, with a nod to us, began singing 'Route Nationale 7', equally iconic in that part of the world. At the far end of the room Mme Gossuet was vigorously defending her soup recipe. The mayor passed among the rowdy tables with a presentation bottle of brandy, a contented smile on his face.

'You are the first English ever to attend this occasion,' he said, laying his hand on Elizabeth's arm.

'May it continue forever.'

'I doubt it. These are the last of a remarkable generation. From now on, boom-shaka-boom-boom, I think.'

Just before we set out for the dinner, Jean-Yves had strolled into the courtyard, wearing his work overalls. He asked me what we planned to do about the garden Mme Elizabeth so much desired. From corner to corner there was a fall of nearly three metres. I mumbled something about terraces and he asked me to sketch what I had in mind.

'C'est pas du gâteau,' he murmured, holding out his hand for the envelope I had scribbled on.

When we came home from the old folks' dinner, he and two young boys, working only with a tractor and trailer, had gone to the quarry a dozen times and spread enough sand to create a three-tier garden. It was the most spectacular act of kindness and generosity either of us had ever experienced, in France or anywhere else, all the more wonderful for being unbidden. Jean-Yves refused payment with a stony hauteur but then relented a very little.

'You could perhaps help my children with their English,' he suggested.

'But you have given up nearly a whole day to do this for us.'

'You are neighbours,' he said, still stiff and unsmiling. He glanced back at his handiwork. 'It looks well. If your husband will lower the height of the walls – you will see I have made a mark in blue chalk – we can use the stones he pulls down to make some plant beds. Herbs are an obvious choice.'

'And flowers.'

'As you wish.'

And then he was gone, sparing himself from any more gushing from us.

'They love you,' I said.

'I told him yesterday that Philippa was coming in the summer. With the children. Also Sophie, Jennie and Alfie. And Thomas.'

'All at the same time?' I cried, aghast.

There were just over 300 people in our commune, which goes a long way towards explaining the general matiness and interaction we enjoyed. What we did not have was a single touristical attraction. The motte-and-bailey castle had been haphazardly inspected and the Mayor of Siecq commissioned a pageant, to which we were all invited. He and his wife hired their robes from a costumier and the cast of loyal peasants made dresses from sacks. Their menfolk sported huge Asterix moustaches. The story the pageant told was wildly ahistorical and ended with a girl in a see-through nightie being spirited away by motorbike.

There were swimming holes dotted about a short drive away, and a lake that had once been a quarry. Its appeal was enhanced by a few shabby-looking pedalos and – much more importantly – excellent *frites*. It attracted what later became known as *les exclus* – the unemployed and the unemployable. If you liked to share your swim with the tattooed and shaven-headed, seldom if ever seen on the streets, this was the place.

It was not likely to entrance four young children. We booked a week in a holiday camp on the Ile d' Oleron and backed it up by buying a fifteen-metre diameter pool which we erected on the second of the terraces Jean-Yves had made us. Rene Boucherie was dismayed. He came round with stories of children being drowned in paddling pools and the awful consequences of something called hydrocution, from which at least one teenager a week died, as reported in the *Sud-Ouest*. *Tous les gars du village* would congregate somewhere, fill themselves with beer and braggadocio and then jump from a handy bridge into the river. For one unlucky lad in ten thousand the shock would hospitalise him – hence hydrocution. Rene attributed these holiday accidents to the malign nature of water itself, its deceptive powers and hungry appetite for innocent young lives. He begged me to empty the pool.

'Just at the moment, the children are with their mothers on the Île d'Oléron.'

'Oh, *les pauvres!*' he cried, wringing his meaty hands in anguish.

There are eight communes on this sandy holiday island, supporting a permanent population of about 19,000. Once, all the traffic was from Oléron to Paris, for the mainstay of the economy was oysters, some millions of which were sent north over the nineteenth and twentieth centuries. But tourism – and the conversion of the Nationale 7 into an autoroute – reversed the trade. The beaches are huge, the tides predictable and in August particularly the weather approaches heatwave intensity. L'Île d'Oléron may lack style or film-star glamour but that is its greatest attraction: it is cheap, classless and frenetic. The disco tune that is that year's beach anthem is played every five minutes: the alleys between the camper-caravans are littered with empty suntan bottles, lolly sticks and lost or broken flip-flops. The island is connected to the mainland by bridge and as you drive across, you have the uneasy feeling that only a few more cars will tilt the balance and tip everything into the sea in one glorious cascade of tents and campers, *frites* and hotdogs, transistor radios and Fanta bottles. In short, it is holiday heaven.

The second week of their stay, we brought them all back to Breuil and threw a sort of garden party for the neighbours. Jean-Yves's children played for a while in the pool, watched by their grandfather and admonished by him every half minute. The English – and the two Americans – had a different idea of how to enjoy themselves, which was to test the pool to destruction. It ended up with rocks being thrown in and scoops of sand flung into people's faces. The water turned milky and unappealing. Michael and Xavier were withdrawn. French lips began to purse. There was only one way to change the mood. I picked Phillipa up and flung her in; and, a little later, Sophie.

A few days later, after they had left, Liz and I went to a *café tabac* I greatly admired and sat in silence among the card players as the purple dusk rolled gently down the hill and the last faint breeze of the day ruffled the leaves. The place had a thirties feel to it – brown and scruffy, lit by neon, except for the bar itself, which was decorated by winking lights. *La patronne*, a woman in her sixties, sat on a high stool watching her clientele and accepting the handshakes of people who came in with a silent nod of welcome. Her employees, the waitresses, were burly women in their forties with broad hips and only the faintest of smiles. She herself was thin and bony, with piled-up hair.

'It's like something from a Simenon novel,' I suggested. 'All these people know the score, they have that weary acceptance that this is how it is and must be. For them.'

'Is weary the right word?'

'They're like Maigret himself, unexcited, calm, I don't know, pacific.'

'Pacific is better. And male. This is a very male place. That's why you like it.'

I leaned across the table and held out my hand. After a few moments she took it. Her mood was shaky. I smiled.

'You and me, girl. It's only ever about you and me.'

The pressure of her hand increased faintly.

'Yes, with the usual reservations.'

There was a car park opposite the café. As we walked to our car, I saw that her cheeks were wet with silent tears.

11

Picnics and Flea Markets

As we grew older, it is my impression that we talked more and more – about films and actors we admired, astronomy and (more hesitantly) particle physics – both of these last late-onset enthusiasms. And then again, other people's relationships, the very long list of mountebanks and scoundrels in party politics, shade-loving plants, how to accelerate decay in compost heaps, small-town America. The ineffable Blair as a wedding organiser, flight steward, under-butler, holiday camp entertainer, white-collar criminal. We talked about nurseries and show gardens, the sociology of floral tributes taped to lamp-posts at the site of car crashes. Or again, more fractiously, how to tune digital radios, record programmes to video, set the timer on the boiler. It amused her that I made such a hash of using the microwave, the dishwasher and washing machine, or that I refused to cook to a printed recipe. It amused me when, fresh from watching a *Horizon* programme, she discovered an extra-terrestrial object stationary over the neighbouring roofs, one that only appeared in wet weather.

'Eric is back,' she would observe, with perhaps a little too much calm.

'Can we say for certain his mission is to spy on two fairly harmless humans with nothing much to say?'

'He has his reasons, I imagine.'

'Perhaps if we put a curtain up at the bathroom window he'd lose interest?'

'Who was it said that since we couldn't be overlooked, there was no need?'

'That was before the intergalactic peeping tom turned up.'

On windy nights, Eric's whole spaceship would thrum like a javelin in flight.

'He's transmitting.'

We finally traced him to a horizontal radio antenna two streets away, glistening when it rained, thrumming in windy conditions and lit intermittently by the security lamps of a neighbouring property, which went on and off according to who was visiting – or simply walking by.

A mystery much nearer to home – in fact across the length of our two gardens – was the man (or woman) who each night illuminated a first-floor back bedroom piled high with boxes and papers but otherwise devoid of furniture. A bare electric bulb hung from the ceiling. Nobody came into the room, nobody left it. The light came on at dusk and was still burning at three or four in the morning.

'This is the house of Dr Banarjee,' I explained, 'of Calcutta and Trinity College, Cambridge. The smallest Fellow of All Souls ever to be elected. He is working on prime numbers.'

'What's in the boxes?'

'The fruits of his research.'

'Weedy,' she decided. 'It is the bedroom of a woman called Elspeth Underwood. The boxes contain drafts of her autobiographical novel, as yet untitled. The story spans all five continents. It runs to 2,000 pages. Half of those are in Mandarin Chinese.'

'She writes by hand, of course?'

'With one of those tortoiseshell fountain pens, yes. She makes her own ink.'

It is so very difficult to replicate the thousands of hours spent talking to each other, except to claim for the experience an intimacy greater by far than sex. If ever we said anything profound or deep, anything that illuminated the human condition in a sudden lightning strike, I have forgotten it. (That is also true of most sex.) Something better was happening, lumpy though it was at times. We communed.

Every morning Liz listened to the radio in the bathroom (the Bath Chronicles) and came downstairs with something worth reporting. Every night we watched *Channel 4 News* together. From these sources we tried to reconstruct what was actually happening in the world, which was to say where the power cables ran. It goes without saying that almost everything we ever thought was a luxury opinion, originating in membership of the privileged minority, not uttered or shaped by the overwhelming majority, the people we met in shops or pubs, or fixing the wayward household equipment. They had things to say we had barely thought.

'I will not let my wife wear jeans,' an unwary AA man advised Liz.

'Poor woman. How weak she must be.'

'She respects my point of view.'

'That's more or less what I meant.'

All this while photographs of her family descended like Perseid showers, at first filed in some sort of order, later on stuffed any which way in the bottom drawer of a military chest: New Mexico mingling with St Ives, Bristol with Breuil. Mountains, hot springs, beaches where the trees in the background all leaned into the wind at the same angle, romantic cafés, unidentified Roman ruins. Interspersed with these were photographs I had taken in India, the Sudan, Cairo, Dakar, all of them completely uninformative and depressing beyond words. We were not memorialists in that way. Given a camera, Liz would quite deliberately place her thumb over half the lens. The pink blob indicated that she was there at the time and there was nothing more she wished to say.

It was Sophie who inaugurated a memorial picnic to honour Eilean's memory. As many as twenty turned up year on year and held a general conversazione (and in a small way sandwich competition). Among the first venues chosen was Kew Gardens. Liz went alone that year and finding it hard to manage a sprained ankle, bought a broom handle from a hardware store on the way and appeared like Charlton Heston in *The Robe*, or more prosaically, Baden-Powell on Brownsea Island. This accidental theatricality was later topped by her ex-husband who arrived one year in explorer tweeds with Thomas following along with a Harrod's picnic basket, much like John Hanning Speke's favourite porter. This took place at the final venue chosen, Old Sarum, an ambiance much to Liz's taste because of the number of trees to be studied from a prone position and perhaps pleasing to Eilean's spirit as well, as being somehow or other suggestive of a more gracious and monied way of life.

What the picnic actually described – apart from Sophie's good nature in convening it – was a yearly get-together of some mildly eccentric *Daily Telegraph* readers.

'It all seems pretty harmless to me,' Liz's brother objected.

'That's because you can't hear what people are saying. Or not saying.'

'I never supposed for a moment that we had to say something interesting. You're asking an awful lot. Do those sandwiches contain meat?'

'You object to meat?'

'No! On the contrary!'

'The game pie is ours. From the Oxford covered market.'

'It looks pretty unequivocal,' he said approvingly. He ate a slice, cupping his free hand under his beard, knees up under his chin. It was the year of the bright orange beret, which, as a former Royal Marine officer, he wore with total indifference to its colour – then stretched out on the grass, talking to Liz about Wagner. Or indeed anything else she might want to mention. I talked to Dick Stamp, one of Terry Stamp's brothers, as good-looking as the actor and ten times as ribald. I only met him once a year at the picnic but he had my number.

'I suppose it's a big step up for you, mixing with the nobs. Social mobility, they call it. Only in England, eh?'

Just as we were the first English couple to attend the *Troisième Age*, so were we the country's sole represent-atives at the *Quatorze*, celebrated at the edge of a field under the partial shade of massive blackthorn hedges. Ten trestle tables were erected and we sat on benches waiting for something to happen. In time bread was issued and a wiry old man with forearms like tree roots passed the length of the tables, chucking down shallots with the soil still clinging to them. At once every man leaned forward and fetched his pruning knife from his pocket, top and tailing the shallots in two or three strokes. After the bread, red wine in plastic bottles. Finally, slices of rillete the thickness of a good-sized paperback. Everybody knew very well that these were from tins of the same but in every year we attended, the rillete was discussed with a sort of forensic rigour. Maybe a little too much salt but then again some people preferred it that way. Madame Audebert was famous for her salt, though Madame Tixier used hardly any, etc. etc. Back and forth, as the men ate their shallots on the point of their knives and the children were given crusts of bread dipped in wine.

The picnic always ended with the mayor passing along the tables, offering each male communard a digestif of cognac. He wore his sash of office, as befitted a civic occasion, but was far more distinguished among his fellow republicans by his tweed jacket and tie, grey flannels and town shoes. His family had been stonemasons in this little commune for over four hundred years. M. le Maire was universally admired for his calm and lack of pomposity. He was a communist by political adherence but a Charentais first and last.

For the first time ever, the roads of the commune were to be given names and the houses numbered. The mayor gave to this task his grave attention and not a little dry wit. For example, opposite Paulette Ayraud's house, where the accursed Parisians had their holiday home, was a weed-strewn mounting block, set there for the benefit of horsemen who had long since ridden off into eternity. Paulette now lived – greatly to her liking – in l'Impasse des Trois Marches. Our own property was bounded by the short lane that led to Jean-Yves' property. It entered official records as l'Impasse Dujardin, so immortalising Gaston of that name, the man who wanted to build a plane.

In Paris, of course, the *Quatorze* always turned the city upside down by the demands made on it by the *defilé*, the parade of every arm of the military, costing half a million euros to stage. We were more modest in our commune but no less patriotic. It was less than a picnic – for example, I never saw anyone bring their own supplementary food or wine – but at the same time greater than a casual gathering. There was no drunkenness or misbehaviour. The commune took their cue from the Mayor. Attending the *Quatorze* was a civic requirement but followed a deeper principle that seems to be embedded in the French mentality. It was the proper thing to do.

As M. le Maire approached the end of the table, a very young girl we had seen from time to time in the tiny supermarket was feeding her baby. She rearranged her T-shirt to hide her breast, not out of any embarrassment, but respect. Gerard Pasquet smiled.

'*Qu' elle est mignone, la petite Lola,*' he said, offering his little finger for the child to clutch.

Every weekend in summer, in one or other village, there would be a *brocante*, a flea market of household goods and the scourings of cellars and barns. There were few dealers – that is to say, interlopers. Local people sold sheets and children's shoes, T-shirts, crockery; but also First World War medals and helmets, Mémé's yellowing library of romantic fiction or perhaps her son's collection of *l'Histoire* and her grandson's pop annuals. All the furniture from the region had long gone, the best of it to America. What was left was the modest bits and pieces of what had been a whole life. I once bought twenty years of the business correspondence of a single-pump garage in some godforsaken hamlet for ten francs. There were more substantial treasures to be had. Together we bought a set of four dozen nineteenth-century wine glasses in various sizes; unmatched Limoges plates and – seized on with a cry of joy from Liz – three zinc watering cans.

In the bigger communes, these *brocantes* were held on the market square, where the mood was boisterous. The hunt might provide a horn trio or glum youths a thrash band. Anyone selling a wind-up gramophone would of course demonstrate it with the playing of shellac records (once, thrillingly, Sibelius; on another occasion Mario Lanza). But the most appealing events were tucked away in woods and fields – quiet, peaceable affairs where many of the *exposants* were elderly and the hours passed slowly. At one of these Liz sat under a lime tree with an old man, talking to him about gardening.

'To grow flowers, they all thought I was mad. Just like you, where you live now, you'll find a few pots of geraniums and maybe a lavender or two. But of course, to attempt anything bigger would be unusual. Where you live in England, it is, I know, very different.'

He rummaged around under his chair, where the dog slept, and produced half a dozen illustrated British seed catalogues from the sixties and seventies, turning the pages slowly for Liz to inspect, as might a stamp collector share his passion with an interested stranger.

At Marsac, just outside Angoulême, there was an annual *brocante* that attracted more than 1200 stallholders. For all but three days of the summer, we knew the place as a swimming hole and café-restaurant that was child-friendly and determinedly old-hat. The owner of the ramshackle wooden café turned out to be the proprietor of the surrounding fields. He was an imposing old man with brusque manners who wanted to brag about his annual dog show and motorcycle convention. The *patronne* of the café was as calm as he was noisy. If one arrived at the right time of the day, when the place was empty, she could be found swimming naked save for her knickers, the pale skin of her back and legs lighting up the water, turning it from dark green to eau de nil. If she was swimming, it was the thing to do to climb the three or four steps to the café verandah and sit with one's back to the river, waiting for her to appear dressed and with hair like rats tails, with the faintest of sardonic smiles.

'You are tourists?' the old man demanded one day.

'We have a house in Breuil.'

'You're German?'

'English.'

'The English always complain about the toilets.'

'And the Germans?'

'Who knows what arrangements they make about such things?'

He passed us a flyer about the upcoming *brocante*.

'Bigger than anything in Paris. The Parisians, poor devils, drive down here to see how it should be done. We have three or four thousand visitors a day. For three days. From all over. Including,' he added with plonking sarcasm, 'Breuil.'

He was not overselling the event. There were restaurants, wine stalls, *buvettes*, artisanal bakers and oyster bars, all punctuating heaps of junk and jumble that crammed four enormous fields right up to the surrounding maize. A tractor dragged red and yellow carriages around the connecting aisles. The smell of its exhaust mingled with that of burnt sugar, barbeque smoke, crushed grass and old carpets. What was on offer was bewildering. Books, clothes, toys, fabrics, every kind of kitchen dish and pot going back a century and a half; the spare parts of cars and tractors, medals, musical instruments, antique televisions, jukeboxes. The man who played the soprano sax to advertise his Sidney Bechet memorabilia was flanked by a shyly smiling stallholder with a collection of several thousand disposable lighters. A few yards further on, an old lady displayed staggeringly beautiful examples of nineteenth-century lace. Next to her, a man with early bicycles and children's pedal cars. It was a happy, self-organising bedlam of men who went home with fishing rods, cow mangers, rustic poles, rolled carpets, leading a family retinue encumbered with plastic bags and newspaper wrappings. Among them, young couples intending to furnish their new apartment with Benares trays or Raoul Dufy prints, stuffed toys and brass measuring scales.

And then there were people like me. One year I found an envelope dating from the military expedition to Morocco at the beginning of the century, overstamped with the name of the camp from which it had been sent. It occurred to me to look for others like it and before I left the *brocante*, I had found another eleven. Among the easiest things to collect were the sweetheart postcards of the Great War in which Henri or Jean-Pierre, Alphonse or Didier stood awkwardly in their field uniforms, surrounded by studio hearts and flowers, the cards addressed to girls who were many of them destined to become widows.

Sometimes complete novels suggested themselves from fragments of correspondence sold from the same vendor. Mme Odette was clearly the confidante of a rather dizzy girl we first meet writing from La Rochelle in 1938. We have her account of her boyfriend, who is most often wearing plus fours and has a very beautiful nose. He likes the cinema but not as much as she: he accompanies her when he has the time. He is nonetheless very gallant – or maybe only seems to be, for in a letter from him to Odette at the same Charentais address, we discover that Hélène has frizzy hair and blue eyes, is nothing much to look at and a bit on the plump side. This somehow accounts for the niggardliness of his letters. He is trying to cut a dash and would like to write entertaining letters of a semi-philosophical character to his aunt. (Hélène writes her scrawls in pencil on the cheapest paper). La Rochelle in the summer is an idyll of well-dressed men and their daughters. Perhaps he is being too easily identified as what he is – a clerk – by his association with the bouncy but empty-headed Hélène.

But there are shadows being cast. At Christmas 1939 we discover him in a camp at Dunkirk. His plus fours are a thing of the past. He is understandably nervous, for though France is living through the all-too-brief phoney war, he has been called out of barracks to put down a strike at the port, an event at which shots are fired. The rest of his platoon are Bretons and he finds their speech and mentality hard to understand. It is bitterly cold and he is homesick.

The last of the letters puts her in Paris in April of 1940. She has a job in a warehouse. The romance with Joseph of the plus fours is now a distant memory. Hélène goes to see her screen hero, Clark Gable, in a farrago of nonsense called *Hell Divers*. The film is already eight years old but that does not matter. Gable's character is killed in a crash onto the deck of an aircraft carrier, sad but exalting somehow. He did what a man must do. He fought; and saved his honour.

A month later the Germans walked into Paris unopposed.

It is all too easy to sentimentalise these adventures and make of Charente Maritime a little unregarded idyll. So it was for us; but not all our visitors found in it what they were looking for. Stan Barstow came out to see us, stayed an hour or two in the house and then retreated to the Hôtel du Commerce. We were too dusty and haphazard and there was only so much to be said about floor tiles and *plac-au-plâtre*. He asked – perfectly understandably – to be taken to some of the better restaurants of the region, which we were at a loss to identify. We took him instead to Saintes, which, in the middle of the nineteenth century, the Virgin Mary visited seventeen times and where there is a Trajan arch and other Roman remains. (More important to me, an excellent second-hand bookshop.)

Stan was a dilatory tourist and difficult guest. What pleased us most about living in Breuil – the neighbours – was, he thought, unimportant detail. After two days, he headed back north. What we should have done was to invite John and Dorothea to meet him at their local restaurant, which only had four tables and where the food was provided by an old lady who cooked for her own pleasure as much as anything else. But our sense of hospitality was sketchy, even in England. In France we had, to his tastes, gone native.

'Well,' Dorothea Alcock commented briskly, 'I can't say I know too much about him. Does he like Roger Peyrefitte? That's a pretty good test of most things literary, I always think.'

'Based on?'

'His first novel, *Les Amitiés Particulières*. A work of art, d'you see?' She laughed at my discomfiture. 'Come on! Can you imagine reading a wonderful novel about buggery published in 1945 after four years of mucking about in Bletchley Park with the Führer's more dangerous dark desires?'

'I have never heard of this author,' John said grandly. He meant of course Stan. And then, incorrigibly, 'There are of course two booksellers in Saintes. As well as M. Charbonnet, who deals from home. I'm very surprised you didn't know that.'

'Brian says his friend buys wine according to its price. The more expensive the better, in his opinion.'

'Oh well!' John crowed, slapping his thigh in delight. 'There is nothing more to be said! No wonder he made his excuses and left!'

A far more enthusiastic guest was the poet Pete Morgan, who came out to write a radio series with me, in which a poet not completely unlike himself writes his autobiography, based only on the mailshots that come through the letter box, his commonplace book and the poems that come to him as a consequence. Pete, a veteran of the New Year's Eve parties, was one of the kindest, most gifted writers I knew, not from a solid base of conviction and study, but perpetually renewed wonder. He was, as a television producer once said of him, the world's oldest teenager.

'Just look at that man delivering water, Brian,' he said to me once outside a French supermarket. 'Hundreds of bottles of water! Thousands, even, every day. What must he dream about at night?'

The world of the *brocante* might as well have been invented for Pete. He roamed about, long-legged and aristocratic-looking, with hardly a word of French, picking up and putting down things like old keys, military shakos, sheet music, tin mugs. He was, as poets must be, penniless. At one place I stood him a beer and told him the story of a football commentator who mused on the burly French international, Patrice Loko: 'He can carry the piano downstairs all right but when he gets it there, does he know how to play it?'

'That's why you're here!' he exclaimed at once. 'That's worth all the effort you've put in! We are bloody clever, you and I, but we could never have written that line. Oh, I am green with envy. It's everything you said it was, you lucky bugger! And then to have the incredibly beautiful Liz to talk to about it – it is what Boucherie *père* insists it is, your own *p'tit coin du paradis.*'

Earlier in the day he had coaxed Rene into repeating this phrase until he had its pronunciation off by heart. When he left to go home, I noticed he had collected all the corks from wine we had chosen together at fourteen francs a bottle. It triggered a memory from the time we had first worked for regional television together in an arts show he presented. There was a poem in it about throwing a piano over a cliff. We could not afford to film at the coast and threw our piano from the first floor of a house due to be demolished next day. After it had shattered, Pete crawled in the wreckage collecting up all the lead counterweights of the keyboard's action.

'They're not worth much, Pete, mate,' one of the crew called, derisively. He looked up from the rubble, wearing his most cautionary expression.

'I am not a scrap metal merchant,' he said. 'These are the dumb audience to "Für Elise". Or, if you like, "Sing As We Go". They have heard wonders.'

12

The Green Tunnel

The lifestyle to be found in *la France profonde* leads to one of the great prizes of social life anywhere: the sophistications (and virtues) of a companionable respect, or what the English once called manners. For example, it would have been unthinkable in our neck of the woods to enter a shop or bar without shaking hands with everyone in it, whether you knew them or not. It was a courtesy that might be lamentably absent in Northern France but for us was a commonplace. A colleague of Paul and Callie's once burst in on tea at Lucette Daniaud's and began talking to them in English about some problem that had arisen with a concert to be given that night.

'Does this young woman never shake hands on entering a room?' our hostess asked me, amazed.

Paul himself, invited by Milhat to meet the mayor of an adjoining commune, turned up at his house in a vest and nylon running shorts. He was shown into a sitting room with leather couches and Indian rugs. By the time he had realised the social gaffe he'd made he was already being pressed, with exquisite manners, to a twenty-year-old cognac.

Elizabeth's birthday was in August and so always celebrated in France. There was a bittersweet element to the day – she wanted to be happy there but did not – could not – give to the house the wholeheartedness that still existed in me. Luckily, I did not have the money to make dramatic improvements and in any case we were not particularly homemakers, there or in England. The place was comfortable but not specially appealing. Pictures helped and a delivery of furniture from England, but we were not the kind of people featured in design magazines, who could turn base metal into gold by restoring an old sewing machine to new use as a wine rack; or repainting a worm-eaten Provençal meatsafe in Van Gogh colours and making it an ingenious space for books on photography and artisanal pottery.

However, Pierre Milhat had been right about one thing: once the barns had gone and the walls lowered, what had been Gaston's forbidding concrete and limestone yard became a model walled garden. The terracing Jean-Yves had created encouraged some adventurous planting, for example a fig tree that found its roots in the sump that had once been the run-off to the cow byres and a walnut that did its best to prosper in a foot or so of imported soil. The two holes that Roger and I had dug were homes to a catalpa and an apple tree. We bought further sections of concrete pipe, enough to create a little township round the well-head.

All that was imaginative about the garden came from Liz and soon enough became her signature statement.

There was nowhere else like it for miles around. The Parisians who took the house opposite Paulette Ayraud hired a man to mow the lawn and plant the borders with annuals just before their arrival. Three weeks later they were gone. The flowers wilted and died behind locked gates three metres high.

If there was a problem with our own garden, it was that it was in full sunshine most of the day. Evening watering, which I liked doing, saw the plants shudder like schoolgirls.

I had once or twice noticed a *tonnelle* in the gardens of falling-down cottages that dated from an earlier and more leisurely age. The principle was simple enough – an arched frame, the roof of which, over time, supported a heavy thatch of *vigne vierge*, creating shade and cool. In short, a green tunnel, leading most often to the front door. A kilometre or so away from us there was a metalworker who undertook to make me one in time for Liz's birthday. I borrowed a pickaxe from Jean-Yves to make the footings for the uprights, of which there were eight. I measured three or four times, he once. He then drove up the hill to study the drawings and returned to measure again, holding out his hand for the pickaxe in silent reprehension. The *tonnelle*, which was four metres long, was fabricated from inch-diameter steel tubes and braced with bar iron. It was, Jean-Yves explained, hopelessly flimsy. Which was to say, in his terms, un-French. When it arrived from the work-shop, I was on no account to touch it without his permission.

He was right. To move the thing from the lorry to the site required eight people – himself, his father, and six old men I had never seen before, all of them with yellow

Gitanes stuck to their lower lips. It was generally agreed that the structure might be alright for Parisians, or Arabs, or people like that, but had no place in Breuil. At which Liz came out and explained very crisply that it was her birthday present, she thought it of excellent design and fabrication and was sure it would give many years of satisfaction.

'You are the people who write books?' a gnarly old Gitane croaked, as if a light bulb had been suddenly switched on inside his head. 'I have heard of you. You buy your melons from my wife.'

There was more discussion, most of it in thick Charentais argot and it was decided at last to give the *tonnelle* the benefit of the doubt. Since we only had to carry it a dozen metres, I couldn't see what the problem was.

'No,' Jean-Yves agreed, tart. 'You can't. It's the welds. If we don't do this right, you will have wasted your money.'

The melon-seller's husband patted me on the back. 'Go and kiss your wife,' he suggested. 'Wish her a happy birthday. And rest easy, *mon vieux. En France, tout est possible.*'

So began a master class in how to turn a bright idea into a finished object. First, the holes I had dug were judged too shallow. Nor had I allowed for a slight fall in the ground. A spirit level and ten-metre tape were called for. Every decision taken was the outcome of lengthy debate.

'For all the trouble they're taking over it, it still looks a bit like a bus shelter,' Liz observed.

'Don't you start. Next year it will be the shadiest spot in Breuil. You will have to put on a cardigan just to go and sit there.'

'Shouldn't you be out there supervising?'

'Are you joking? I haven't been allowed to go near it since it arrived.'

For which I was secretly grateful. A year earlier, I had collapsed the third and fourth vertebrae of my spine, trapping the brachial nerve. It was the first medical calamity of my life. I could barely use my left arm for two months and the pain in my neck and back was almost unbearable. I spent four days in St James's hospital in Leeds, undergoing tests. A pleasant Indian doctor passed what he promised were microvolts up the nerves to my arm, the effect of which was directly comparable to having an outraged rabbit run through the veins to hide in my armpit. The doctor glanced at the dials on the equipment and made a hasty adjustment. Next day, in what I hoped was an unrelated test, I was examined for spinal injury.

'I am going to pass a needle into your spine. You can if you wish see the procedure on a monitor. I must caution you not to move, or cough, or even speak, however, because otherwise you run the risk of paralysis.'

'I would like to follow things on the monitor,' I mumbled.

'Good man.'

Just after the needle was inserted, an unseen person came into the room.

'Dunc, there's a phone call for you.'

'Not now.'

'It's your girlfriend. There's a problem with the wedding.'

I lay looking at the impossibly long needle, which showed as a dark shadow in a greeny fog. I was immobilised with terror. There were several seconds of silence.

Then Dunc's youthful and guileless face appeared from nowhere, upside down and very close.

'I'll just take this call. Shan't be a moment. Don't move a muscle.'

That evening Fat Boy, the ward orderly, came and sat at the end of bed. He had a baby's plump features, offset by a buzzed-up haircut and single hoop earring.

'Don't tell me. Motorcycle accident. Am I right? Bit old for that game, aren't you?'

'I was sleeping on my son's floor without a pillow.'

'Strewth,' Fat Boy said, impressed. 'Lucky you had someone to help you.'

'He lives in Brighton. That's where it happened.'

'How'd you get back here?'

'By train. Standing all the way.'

'Was that wise?'

'As it turns out, no.'

Fat Boy studied me with genuine pity in his eyes.

'You live alone,' he decided.

'No.'

When I did get home that terrible night, Liz thought I had been mugged, or shot. She was all for calling the police. She had a sketchy idea of first aid learned from classes at school. But then, these had been taught by a retired brigadier whose speciality was demonstrating breast bandaging to the more compliant girls.

'I don't know what to do,' she wailed. 'Shall I call Brian Poe in New Mexico?'

'Open a bottle of wine. I need to be drunk.'

The follow-up to the hospital investigations was an appointment with the consultant, scheduled on Christmas Eve. It was perfectly clear that the outpatients' clinic was already in holiday mood. Up and down the corridor there was raucous laughter and the sound of nurses scampering about like meerkats. The consultant was a young Australian in the image of Shane Warne. He pointed to a plastic column hanging dolefully from a beechwood gibbet.

'Know what that is?'

'It's a spine.'

'Know how it works?'

'No.'

'Neither does anyone else and don't let them tell you different. Come and have a drink.'

The problem recurred regularly. I found it difficult to raise my arms higher than my shoulders and had great trouble turning my head to the right. The children bought me a mountain bike for my sixty-fifth birthday and I had to give it up before I had cycled twenty miles: it was too dangerous to ride. Even in France, along largely empty lanes, I could not manage. Rene Boucherie noticed the condition and passed on his concerns to his son. Jean-Yves immediately consigned me to the rubbish dump of human beings who have to be mollycoddled through life. Not only was I constitutionally inept at all the things he held dear, I was, by injury, dangerously maladroit. That was how in the siting of the *tonnelle* I had become a mere supernumerary.

Liz, too, had her misadventures. Leaning over the gas stove to stir a pot one lunchtime, she set alight her long muslin shift. I ran into the kitchen just as she was sheeted in flame, screaming and trying to run water to douse herself. I pulled her away from the stove and ripped away her shift and bra. We rushed to Cognac, taking with us Paulette Ayraud, who was quite certain we would never find the hospital. (It was widely signposted all over town in letters a foot high.) It was the hospital where her husband had died and while we waited for Liz to be examined, she ran through all the other fatal emergencies she had witnessed. She pointed to Liz being wheeled in a chair across the interjunction of a corridor.

'When they get the chair out like that, it's always bad news.'

In the waiting room was a boy in his twenties who had dived into a holiday-camp swimming pool which had only a foot of water in it. He had a broken nose, two black eyes and a huge gash to his scalp but sat reading a motor-cycle magazine, just as if he was waiting for a consultation with a doctor about constipation. After a few minutes, however, he leaned forward and was copiously sick between his bare legs. I went to find someone on the medical staff to report this. The corridors were empty and I found I was shaking with fear. At last an elderly nurse approached and seizing me by the elbow escorted me back through the swing doors.

'Look at the mess he's made,' Paulette said indignantly as he too was put in a wheelchair and carted out. By way of riposte he was sick again. None of this calmed the mind.

'Well,' Rene Boucherie said when I returned that night without Liz, 'you did the right thing by tearing off her clothes. She will be back tomorrow and then you'll see. The calm of this little corner of paradise and a good soup every evening will set things right. Where did you learn what to do?'

'In the army,' I said, still shocked and confused.

'Of course. I had forgotten.'

In Kenya, as a National Service subaltern, I had held a wounded African askari in my arms waiting for him to die. But this was worse.

'I was a bloody fool and deserved what I got,' she said when she did come home. 'But I knew I could depend on you.'

'You mean that?'

'You are brave, in your way. I am not.'

'Would you like to go home?'

'It will be a lot more painful travelling than staying put. Where did you get this soup?'

'Arlette Boucherie brought it round this morning.'

'Oh, bloody hell. It's so terrible being old.'

'You're not old. Nobody thinks of you as old.'

'Well, I am. And where did you get this blouse?'

'In Cognac this morning. Before I picked you up.'

I had pulled it off the rack in a shop dedicated to young fashion. It was lavender blue and four sizes too large but made from what looked like knitted cobwebs.

'It's perfect.'

Maybe we were getting old, something I had not bargained for. It put a new complexion on things. One of the more obstinate opinions Liz held was that alternative medicine was systematically overlooked by researchers and obscurantist doctors. Great things could be achieved with homoeopathic medicines. Nor had it ever been convincingly disproved that the alignment of the stars and planets had things to say about us that general practitioners also ignored. (In this she was egged on by Deb [Spranger] Gill, formerly of Dames, who cast the astrological charts of the entire family. I was especially badly aspected and the prize went to Sophie, whose star signs much resembled Stalin's.

Only a lack of opportunity for ruthless murder and the matter of gender separated them. Sophie was what Stalin might have been had he been a woman.)

Liz had so many hares running like this that in times of good health it seemed merely an endearing foible. But as she grew older, she came to depend more and more on alternative medicine. Both in England and France, tubs of evening primrose, chellated magnesium and the like piled up. This led to a famous exchange with our friend Anthony Hands, a biochemist turned archaeologist and (in my experience) an awesome contrarian.

'In my opinion, all that's required for general good health is a pork chop eaten every lunchtime,' he once said. Liz rounded on him.

'Anthony, how can you say that? What on earth makes you say that?

'On the argument that you never see a pig going into Holland & Barrett,' he chortled.

She did not like it. I had a marked unwillingness to define good health or bad. It frightened me a little that we seemed to be talking about it more and more, in line with the general cultural drift, to be sure, but tied to our own feeble ailments – a blocked nose, feelings of lassitude, loss of appetite, restless leg. Quite suddenly, I found I was living with a full-blown health nut. The tubs of vitamin supplements and extracts of this or that began to pile up. The bathroom cupboard could not hold them all. Thomas, who lived in the direst parts of downtown Liverpool, sent Chinese herbal teas from backstreet shops; dried wonder vegetables unknown to conventional medicine – and Tiger Balm, to be applied to the temples for anything short of actual death.

One night, when we sitting out under the leafless *tonnelle* – very much like two pensioners waiting for a bus – Liz threw me a small hand grenade.

'Rene Boucherie was telling me the other day about a *raboteur* who has done wonders for Arlette's knees.'

'And?'

'This man got a quadraplegic cow to walk and you can't have a better recommendation than that. I thought he might help your back.'

'Is he strictly unqualified in any actual branch of medicine? Because I don't want to waste my time on a conventional quack.'

'Rene knows about these things.'

'We are talking about the same man who asked me whether we had the Halle-Bopp comet in England, who assured me there was no such place as East Africa, only North, West and South? The tank gunner from the war with Algeria? That Rene?'

'Yes! The one who can bend horseshoes straight and throw cows through hedges! The one who doesn't have to walk about with a hot water bottle on his neck every couple of months!'

'You are shouting.'

'Yes! I feel like shouting.'

'Elizabeth, there is alternative medicine and there is madness —'

But she was already on the way back into the house.

The *raboteur* lived ten kilometres away. Not every village in France is a potential movie location: nor is every house steeped in romance. M. Charlot lived in a bungalow that would not have been out of place anywhere along the Essex coast. His front garden was an untended wilderness and the paint to his door hung in flaps. There was a galvanised tin porch supported on one side by a brick pier and on the other by a whimsically extemporised yard broom. A brown shadow peered through a glass panel and this turned out to be a receptionist, or possibly the *raboteur*'s wife. I was shown in to a consulting room piled with washing waiting to be ironed and cardboard boxes crammed with newspapers and magazines. Charlot, when he appeared, was a ratty-looking man in nylon trousers and a grubby vest. We shook hands.

I tried to outline the history of my condition. This he waved away as being of no interest. I should undress to the waist and then we would see. He began by tracing the veins in my arms with a none-too-clean thumbnail. Then he swept that day's paper and what appeared to be some tax returns from a table. I was invited to lay face-down in their place.

'Here is the problem,' he said, pressing down on my neck. I yelped. The same brown smudge of a woman appeared with a tray of glasses and a brass bowl half filled with burning charcoal. When I tried to sit up, he held me down by laying his forearm across the small of my back.

'You are an unwilling patient,' he observed.

'That is true. I like to know what is being done to me.'

'Your English doctors no doubt explained what was being done to you in detail and to your complete satisfaction. And do you feel any better for it? I think not. You are an educated man?'

'In England, yes.'

'You are afraid of growing old?'

'Has my spine told you that?'

'But of course,' he rejoined. 'I am going to cup your back. It is not painful. But please keep your opinions to yourself from now on.'

Half an hour later I sat up, feeling very slightly light-headed.

'You have slept.'

'That's not very likely.'

'Just as you wish,' Charlot said with the greatest complacency, lighting a cigarette. He took a small length of red elastic from the floor, wiped it free of dust and knotted it high up on my arm.

'When this falls to your wrist, the treatment will be complete.'

'I will be cured?'

His smile was thinner than a knife-edge. Whether I had slept or not, one consequence of the cupping was that my sense of smell was enormously enhanced. Or maybe it was his cigarette. The whole place stank of sweat and stale cabbage. I passed him his money and, as was required by custom, shook his hand again.

'Well, do you feel any better?' Liz asked when I got home.

'I made friends with his octopus,' I said, pulling off my shirt to show her the reddened circles where the cups had been.

'What is that thing on your arm?'

'Knicker elastic. All included in the price.'

'You can be very hateful sometimes.'

I took both her thin hands in mine and bounced them against my chest.

'Am I really hateful?'

'No,' she said. 'Yes, sometimes. While you were out,

Riffault brought a parcel round. I think it's the books you ordered from Poitiers. Don't you want to open it?'

'Charlot asked me if I am an educated man.'

'Ha!' she gloated. 'Educated, yes. But any wiser than an ox? Well, the jury's out on that one.'

We kissed. The parcel from Poitiers lay on the table between us.

13

La Frairie

In 1889, an Englishwoman in her fifties rang the bell to a hospice in the little town of Gisors, north of the Seine. The male inmates had most of them been brought low by Normandy cider; the women by more subtle despairs. Mrs Weldon, as she introduced herself to the nuns that ran the place, had with her some caged birds, several trunks of papers and a monkey called Titileehee. It was night, she had never met the nuns before in her life – and, moreover, she was a Protestant. Her French was racy and idiomatic and she used it to astound the Mother Superior, who was to understand that she was receiving one of the most put-upon women in all creation. Jeremiah himself was never more afflicted.

She had not come for refuge and certainly not for spiritual instruction. She was here to write a book that would expose the perfidy of the English legal system. In the first instance, something to eat and a room over-looking the garden would be helpful. The nuns need not invite her to join them at their devotions – that side of things was just so much tosh. But she would be grateful for a good supply of ink and paper and some shelves to store her research materials, which turned out to be transcripts of Old Bailey trials, news cuttings, letters and photographs. One of these photographs was of the composer Gounod, looking suitably defensive. She had, she confided cheerfully, gone after him in England with a loaded revolver, only to be arrested by the Birmingham police before she could assassinate the scoundrel.

The parcel from the bookseller contained the fruits of Georgina Weldon's stay at Gisors. It comprised six volumes in once red, now faded pink covers, self-published and printed at Dijon by a man she promised to indemnify from prosecution for the contents of the text. And with good reason. The memoirs could never have been published in England, nor in English, for they were a forest of libels from end to end. Mrs Weldon was a vain, intemperate, often incoherent chronicler of her own life, with a grudge against men, and lawyers in particular. By any measure, her life had been disastrous.

In an unimportant sense, finding her tucked away in the pages of a provincial French bookseller's catalogue was vindication of a lifelong weakness for random book-collecting. I had rediscovered one of the great eccentrics of the nineteenth century, once famous for being famous and among the first of that ilk. Georgina Weldon was so preposterous, so foolhardy, that the social class from which she sprang kept silent whenever her name was mentioned. The fame she felt she deserved was given to her – in a way very familiar to us nowadays – by newspaper proprietors and their editors. She was copy. And like many another celebrity since, she misunderstood the kind of fame on offer. She was poisoned by it and – by the time she pitched up at Gisors – damaged beyond all hope.

At her funeral in 1914 there were only seven mourners. The husband she execrated so bitterly on almost every page of the memoirs was not one of them. Dull, unimaginative, duplicitous Harry Weldon, the husband she had created as if from clay – better still, straw – was a penniless hussar officer when she married him, and now, by some impossibly comic engine of fate, Acting King of Arms in the College of Heralds. Georgina's funeral was the last place on earth he wanted to be that icy January day.

All this was to be glimpsed through a fog of bad French and a manic enthusiasm for detail, the legal minutiae of a disastrous life. But, tangled up with the torrent of libels and catastrophic misjudgements of other people's motives, there was a story to be told of great importance to women in particular. I had a head start on anyone else who might have bought the work in the past: I was reading, in some sense, about my mother.

I wrote a proposal for my agent, who listened sympathetically, laughed immoderately and steered me round the pubs of Notting Hill. I showed him the first chapter, he showed that to a publisher and on Cheltenham Gold Cup day, while drinking in Oxford with other habitués of a Ladbrokes betting shop, he tracked me down to the Red Lion and rang to say that he had secured an advance of five figures. How he found me there, I had no idea.

'He problay go, like, is there a white geezer in there what smoke a stinky old pipe, know what I'm saying?' one of the West Indian crew I hung out with suggested. 'Like he ony bet on long odds? Baldy guy, shit shoes, no style?'

'That must be it.'

''Less he's Sherlock Holmes, know what I'm saying? Why he don't bother to ring your mobile?'

'I haven't got one.'

'Yeah, right.'

My editor's name was Arabella, the first – and last – of my acquaintance. Her trust in me to write a halfway decent book was bracing. I got myself a reading card to the Bodleian Library. The ID photograph that went with it showed a wary-looking pensioner bundled up in a Bundeswehr camouflage jacket with the addition of a Trinity First and Third scarf, my idea of supplementary accreditation. I chose the Upper Reading Room for my investigations, found space at a desk and began to study. Within a month, I became a history bore.

'Did you know that sliding seats were introduced to rowing in 1872?' I asked Liz.

'This has some bearing on the book, does it?'

'I just stumbled across it in the ordinary way we have of doing things down there, you know.'

'Did this Arabella give you the advance just to enjoy yourself?'

'I think she did,' I answered wonderingly.

But she and Arabella were out of the same box, as was made clear at their first meeting. They had the same accent, understood the same niceties.

'You mention Northern Ireland. Was your father an academic?'

'No, he was a soldier.'

'What did he do there?'

'Well, he was more or less in charge of things.'

Arabella's shrewdness (which she concealed as skilfully

as one of Smiley's people) was greater than an invitation to enjoy myself. She wanted me to take myself seriously. And so I did, I think a little to Liz's discomfiture. I put up more shelves and began buying second-hand books through the internet. This was a step in the right direction. In the past I had relied on browsing market town bookshops. Every Thursday in Oxford, I haunted a particular market stall on Gloucester Green. The vendor was Keith Clark, an incomparable bookseller and bibliophile with a stock he changed every week. He was also of unrivalled morosity, a quality in him I liked very much.

'Are any of these books first editions?' an American asked him once.

Keith passed him *Our Common British Fossils: A handbook for students*, published in 1885 and never reprinted.

'There are others,' he said, bleakly. The American held the book in his hands without opening the covers. 'I was thinking more of Salman Rushdie, Ian McEwan, those sort of guys.'

All this while, the disastrous Mrs Weldon was leading me on, scattering paper behind her. In the end, seventeen trunks of evidence (as she saw it) followed her across the Channel. Gounod, who had died at his desk while his wife sewed peaceably in the same room, appeared to Georgina Weldon in séances arranged by her wily servant, whose boyfriend was literate (as she was not). When the couple decamped suddenly, Gounod went with them. What he had to say to her from beyond the grave was in any case nothing but mawkish sentimentality when what she wanted from him was howling remorse at his failure to acknowledge her genius. She wanted the torment of the damned.

'You are the ideal man to write about her,' Liz said one night in France.

'She felt betrayed by almost every man she met.'

'That was at the back of the remark, I suppose. You are giving her your best shot. What else counts?'

Earlier in the evening a hunting owl had paused to study the garden, perched on the branch of a neighbouring tree. It seemed like a good omen.

'Minerva has come to bless my efforts.'

'Or check up on you. Or give you back your Bodleian card.'

Out of the advance for the book, I bought Liz an astronomical telescope. Though we lived in one of the least populated communes in France, where everybody but us went to bed at nine-thirty, there was an unforeseen difficulty with stargazing. One of M. le Maire's improvements to the commune had been to install a street light fifty metres from the house where the road bent a little. Accordingly, the conditions improved dramatically after midnight, when the street light was extinguished. I watched her in silhouette searching for Virgo and Leo over M. Voyer's fields, hunched forward in a chair, pausing from time to time to relight her pipe, considered an affectation in England but utterly unremarked upon in Breuil. My heart ached for love.

Kath and Trev were from Yorkshire and had a very large house on the road to Rouillac. We first met them in the parish church at Beauvais-sur-Matha where Paul's students were giving a concert. I introduced them to John and Dorothea, who had been roped in to make up the numbers.

'And are you also buying a property from these greedy

French peasants?' Kath asked, misreading them for hapless old retirees. Dorothea laughed and asked her from what part of Yorkshire she came. It was a shrewd thrust.

Kath and Trev had made their money from setting up pharmacies in isolated pit villages in the Doncaster area. Good-hearted Kath was given to judge others by the amount of money they could command. Trev was a bit more enigmatic. Like Jean-Yves, the world of material objects posed no threat to him. Singlehandedly, day after day, he was remodelling a former *auberge* to make of it what Kath described as 'the habitation of an English gentlewoman abroad and that's the long and short of it.'

They were flummoxed by Liz, who could have done better for herself all round, in Kath's opinion. She came to Breuil to inspect us. We had no view (their place overlooked maybe ten miles of vineyards on the way to Cognac); no furniture worth speaking of; and a layabout who was writing a book that nobody in their right mind would want to read. She was also staggered by the cheapness of the wine we drank.

'Outside in that car right now are a dozen bottles that we take with us whenever we leave the house. They are worth gold dust, believe you me.'

'You take your wine with you?'

'Whenever we leave the house. You live in Oxford, I understand. Are you graduates?'

'Yes, but not from Oxford.'

'See, I know about you, Liz, from Norma Jacobs. She's read your books and claims to like them. But you –' she said, rounding on me – 'I don't know the first thing about you. Except that you play golf with Norma, or used to.'

Norma Jacobs was the wife of the coroner that Mike

Toft liked to consult at New Year's Eve parties. We did indeed play golf all summer in the days before I bought Gaston's house. I was momentarily translated from a garden in France to the tricky short hole at Skipton Golf Club, where anything we hit off the tee – a club selection of any kind – sent the shot towards mysterious ball magnets hung in the trees, or waiting at the bottom of a small pond. There was silent anguish in our partnership.

'Brian read English at Cambridge,' Liz murmured.

'Oh well,' Kath said crushingly. 'That explains a lot.'

'Liz read English and Philosophy at Leeds,' I said.

'Are these teacups local?' she sniffed.

'From Heal's.'

'And what is that thing out in the garden?'

'A pergola, or the beginnings of one.'

She permitted herself a thin smile of triumph.

'For an English graduate, you want to get your pronunciation right for a start. The word is Perg-Ola.'

'I hadn't heard that.'

'I daresay. Well, I went to Pontefract Girls' Grammar School and was taught English by a woman with two degrees. It's a matter of stresses. Pergola is a word of two syllables: perg and ola.'

There was something about Kath and Trev that harked back to village life in the nineteenth century. She was a noisy, wholly good person who could never quite find her place. Too obvious a target for Thackeray, too minor a character to interest Dickens, she could have come from the pages of Jane Austen, perhaps as a relative of Mrs Bennett. Much as she wished to pigeonhole us, she was too guileless to have it how she wanted. She would introduce me to friends from England with a recapitulation of the pergola story, perhaps to draw attention to the shortcomings of the English Tripos.

'Have you found a reliable local to build you this pergola?' someone asked.

'Oh, he thinks he can do it himself,' Kath said. 'To which Trev says fat chance.'

'I have been half-panelling the sitting room in oak,' he said to no one in particular. 'It looks very well.'

Jean-Yves was of the same opinion as Trev when it came to my abilities. He examined the rustic poles to be used in the making of the pergola and told me that the whole sorry structure would fall down within twenty-five years.

'It will outlive me, then.'

He frowned. Things like this were not to be taken lightly. His pale eyes searched mine.

'How will you fix the cross beams?'

'With nails, I imagine.'

He barked out a laugh, as though I said something so absurd that a lapse in good manners could be excused.

'I think I can find you half a dozen telegraph poles,' he said. 'I will measure and cut them to length for you. It will make a better job.'

'That is kind, but this is something I want to do on my own. For Madame Elizabeth, you understand. I am writing a new book. But I don't want her to think I have forgotten the garden.'

'If you build it with the poles you've bought, it will be memorable,' he promised. 'What is the book you're writing?'

'It's about a madwoman,' I said, simplifying for the

sake of brevity. 'But a very gifted one. On another subject, does it always rain here the first week in August?'

'To do with the high tides, yes. You know, the perturbation of the sea.'

Just as Jean-Yves doubted my ability to build a pergola, so John Alcock was dubious about the chances of my getting a book out of Georgina Weldon.

'You say the text is in French. Are you confident your command of the written language is adequate?'

'Perfectly so.'

'Ha!' he cried. 'Well, we shall see. Is the intended publisher a reputable one?'

'David Beckham has chosen them for his several autobiographies.'

'And who, may I ask, is David Beckham?'

'Of Manchester United and England. The book has his kind of fame as its theme.' And then, in an attempt to head him off, I added this. 'Fame as the self-delusion of the innocent. She was a very wicked woman in her way, but it all sprang from an inability to recognise that one thing is better than another. I don't know what you'd call that.'

'Ignorance,' he said, with his maddening aplomb. 'Which is bliss until you are found out.'

That year's *frairie* was more than usually merry. Arlette Boucherie had been replaced as a councillor by Martine Ayraud. As a consequence she had washed her hands of organising the event. Even attending it was a vexation for her: she sat to one side of the marquee with her arms folded, scowling. Meanwhile, surrounded by helpers, Martine darted in and out of the kitchens, her hair stuck to

154

her skull with sweat, passing us titbits from the meal to come. She had engaged a husband and wife accordion duo to animate the *bal musette* that was to follow the food. Their music was needed long before that.

The commune had been bidden for 8.30, and – forewarned by previous experience – we turned up at 9.15. The first course was served an hour later. The boys of the village were in boisterous mood, singing schoolboy anthems and beating the tables with their fists every time the lights failed. (The committee was having the same old problems with the ovens: the sprite-like Coco Tardy was stationed at the junction box that led from the main feed with his own bottle of wine and a little sack of spare fuses.)

Gerard and Ghyslaine, the accordionists, were hardened veterans of such evenings as this. They were in their forties and utterly imperturbable. Ghyslaine wore cruel specs but had, as Liz noted, very clear and pale skin and a firm chin. Sitting opposite us was a tiny little bald man who lived in Paris and handled the secret archives of the Ministry of Marine.

'If this were a film, Madame Ghyslaine would be played by Julie Andrews,' Liz suggested.

'You are in the right of it,' he exclaimed. 'You are English yourself, madame?'

'I am.'

'You may know my sister. She lives in Liverpool.'

'My son lives in Liverpool. He may know her.'

'*Voilà!*' he said, greatly contented, but, as befitted his profession, not without a secret smile. When the main course finally arrived, she donated her steak to him and later on several glasses of cognac, smuggled to us by Martine. He greatly resembled a French character actor whose name I have forgotten – lively, intelligent and knowing. He was easy to picture scurrying down the corridors of the Ministry to emerge onto the streets of Paris at the magic hour of soft light and long shadows. We found ourselves talking about the Maillol, the cabaret whose neighbour was the Folies Bergère. At the Folies, the scene changes were introduced with the minimum of explanation, followed by a cascade of flesh.

'*Oh, qu'il fait froid maintenant, non?*' that year's ingénue would exclaim to that year's smoothy-boots, in front of a darkened stage.

'*Mais bien sur, cherie,*' he would reply fondly. '*C'est le Pole Nord!*'

At which the lights went up and fifty or so topless girls sauntered on in white fur hats and snowflakes for knickers and a twenty-piece orchestra for accompaniment. The girls at the Folies were contracted to the show for four years, which gave them the confidence to stare down their audience of (largely) German and American tourists with a magnificent hauteur.

At the Maillol, the company was smaller, with a sardonic breeziness that said, 'well, you didn't come here for big production numbers and snowflakes. Here we are, we're down to our last stitch, you can see the sweat glistening on our arms and legs. You've just given the comic the bird, and that's OK, but don't pretend you can belittle this!' Drum paradiddle, four bars in and then the hoofing.

The photographer Brassaï was the recording angel of Montparnasse in the thirties and one night he framed a shot of a cabaret chorus line. Of the six girls, three of them are looking down at their legs to shuck off their stage costume without risking a fall into the orchestra pit.

Two of them, who have already done this, are talking to each other, maybe about men, maybe about last night's supper. They are smiling at each other like young women on a bus. The image is untitled but may have been captured at the Maillol. It is certainly how I remember it from the fifties.

When the meal ended and the *bal musette* began, our friend from the Ministry of Marine rose gallantly and unsteadily and asked Liz to dance. He was no taller standing up than he had been sitting down but turned out to be a fantastic dancer. He and Liz stamped and slid, twirled, she with her sailor's hornpipe, he with more than a little of the Apache about him. They stole the dance floor. The bellowing and banging on tables that had punctuated the meal segued seamlessly into wild cheers and applause. Gerard and Ghyslaine beamed. Martine Ayraud beamed. Arlette Boucherie frowned. Jean-Yves gawped.

We drove home at two in the morning, fell into the house and drank a couple of glasses of Bourgogne to round off the evening. Liz was first in the bathroom and came downstairs to say goodnight in pyjama bottoms and a saggy T-shirt. She stood in the doorway to the *salle de séjour*, looking challenged and spoiling for a fight she knew in her heart would never come.

'When we get back to England,' she said. 'I am going to buy some tap shoes. I have put this off far too long.'

'Brilliant,' I said, jumping up to embrace her. In a week's time she would be sixty-eight years old. And for that I had planned what I hoped would be a big surprise.

14

The Year of the Mobilette

For this particular birthday, I persuaded the man who made us the *tonnelle* to renovate his father-in-law's mobilette and sell it to me with two new tyres and a new saddle. Every child for miles around who was fourteen or over had one of these busy little two-strokes, which could turn thirty kilometres an hour – downhill and with a following wind – into lift-off from Cape Kennedy. Every evening in the hour or so before dusk, the road outside the house was drilled with noise as schoolboys raced each other. No licence was required and the maintenance of the engines was simplicity itself.

On the morning of Liz's birthday, the mobi was delivered by pick-up truck, an additional flourish that almost laid the whole scheme low, for she very naturally assumed the bike was on its way elsewhere and, after shaking hands with M. Voyeron, peered hopefully into the back to see if there was anything else he might have brought along just for her. Voyeron opened the tailgate and ran the mobi down a scaffolding plank. He seemed startled by her whoops of pleasure. We were, after all, foreigners and nobody could say for certain what we were thinking.

Liz did nothing to disabuse him of his views about the English. She asked him how it worked, which for Voyeron was much like asking him how to fill a bath or answer the telephone. Luckily it was one of Jean-Yves' days for keeping an eye on us and Voyeron passed to him the task of fielding questions no child would dream of asking. There followed a sermon, the main burden of which was that riding a bike with an engine on it was utterly against nature. Many French people had such a thing but who was to say they were any happier? Generally speaking, he was sure we would find no great use for it.

'But can you show me again how to engage the gears?'

'The gears?' he bellowed, incredulous. 'There are no gears.'

To go with the mobi, I bought her a visored helmet and a set of maps, big enough in scale to show the local field boundaries and tractor lanes. She was entranced. Later that week I was playing boule with some old boys of the village when one of them lifted his head and swung it round, like a beast in the field.

'Here comes Madame Elizabeth,' he croaked.

At first I could hear nothing because I was listening for the characteristic brrrp! of a boy-racer. But at last, muffled by a stand of oaks, came phut-phut, putter-putter-putter-phut as she passed, her helmet reflecting back the sun.

'She has missed her way,' the melon seller's husband said. 'That's Hubert's maize she's riding through.'

The burst of laughter that followed was an indication that, far from hiding herself away in the landscape, as she had hoped, she was already notorious. I might have helped restore some honour to our reputation by beating these veiny old men when we resumed the game of boules. But at the last Concours, which had attracted eighty or so players competing for prizes like a side of ham, bottles of cognac and the like, Jean-Pierre Ayraud and I had been trounced in the very first round by two boys, the oldest of whom was twelve years old. We were liked in the commune only because there was no saying what foolishness we might commit next.

'What picture is that?' Paulette demanded on one of her visits, pointing to a canvas by Frank Howard.

'It is called *An Aubergine at Midnight*,' I improvised, shaping my hands suggestively in front of Frank's wild slashing blues and blacks.

'The poor man has lost his mind,' she decided. 'But then again, it is exactly the sort of thing you would choose to put on a wall. Is it drugs that has led him to paint like this?'

'Worse,' I said gravely.

We bought saddlebags for the mobi that Liz filled with bottled water and chocolate, scribbling pads and throwaway cameras. As I had guessed, she liked most to travel the field boundaries in search of noble trees and – if it was early enough in the morning – deer. She was in the landscape and of the landscape – but alone. At night she would drink a glass or two of wine, refining the map with pencil markings that indicated loose shale, potholes or in one place 'Snake!!!!'

She quizzed the local children about how to reach neighbouring villages by indirect routes and had the disappointment of finding that they could not give the simplest directions, even by the main road. Florent, Romain and Xavier knew all about Senegal, having had its location drummed into them at school for a year, but had no idea where nearby Loussac was. Nor could they easily point to a map of Europe and identify, for example, Spain or Germany. Their forebears had been dragged out of the fields, enlisted, cuffed round the ear and told to walk to Austerlitz in the shoes they happened to have on their feet – or no shoes at all. They were more travelled than these skinny boys in their T-shirts and nylon shorts.

'Anyway,' the sulky Xavier said, 'grannies shouldn't ride mobilettes.'

He appeared to realise he had given away his father's opinion on the matter and sloped off shortly after.

Florent Naud, the most nervy of the three, blushed red. 'I can run and ask my mother where Loussac is,' he suggested.

'That won't be necessary,' Liz said. Romain, Paulette Ayraud's grandson, winced.

'She is angry with us,' he whispered.

'Not at all. But before you go, show me where Paris is. In which direction?'

There was more panicked semaphoring with their stick-like arms. Later that night, Paulette swung by. The urgency of her visit was indicated by the fact she was still wearing her check slippers.

'Don't even dream of going to Paris on that thing,' she said, pointing at the mobi. 'It's not a good idea – in fact it's probably illegal. And you,' she added, rounding on me, 'sending her off to certain death! Oh, *mon dieu*, when Romain told me what you were planning I felt my heart bounce like this.'

She showed how her heart had bounced by cupping one sagging breast and jiggling.

'Calm yourself, Paulette. I have no plan to visit Paris, or anyway not this week. I was just chatting with Romain about the points of the compass.'

'*Hein?*'

'Where everything is.'

'The sun has got to your head. Places are where they've always been, naturally.'

'Well, you show me in which direction is Paris.'

She looked at me with flashing eyes. 'See what you've done, buying her that? And while we're about it, what's that nonsense you've built out in the garden?'

'A pergola.'

'Oh, next we'll be having a little lake and a rowing boat, I suppose,' she said, brushing away our offer of Fanta, the only thing she would drink when she came to visit. Martine arrived in the doorway, bearing a cardigan. Her mother-in-law put it on immediately.

'They have no idea about the danger from draughts, either. The poor woman could die of pneumonia for all he cares,' she grumbled. 'The door left open all hours of the night.'

'About the mobi, I am actually very timid,' Liz said. 'I don't go fast and I'm always nervous.'

'You are very formidable,' Martine corrected gently. 'Everybody knows that about you.'

As soon as we got back to Oxford, Liz bought a top-of-the-range pair of tap shoes and joined a group that met at the old Social Club in the Cowley Works, where there was a sprung floor that was, as she put it, to die for. She and her elderly posse hammered away at 'Honeysuckle Rose' and 'Tea for Two'. The majority were tubby old dames who had come out for the exercise and to escape line dancing and all that cowboy crap that was so popular on the estates. The tutor was a leggy girl in her thirties who had been in the chorus of a West End show or two. From this gaggle of women – and four arthritic old men – she was determined to make a chorus line. There was to be no backsliding. Homework would be set. It was exactly what Liz wanted. When she came home, she held onto the kitchen counter while waiting for the kettle to boil, practising steps.

'We are doing something from *Mary Poppins* towards Christmas. A routine,' she added, as if to a child. 'It is called "Chimney Sweeps Are Us". I shall need a decent brush.'

'Does it have to be fully functional?'

'Don't you ever get tired of being a smart-arse?'

'When you said "I shall need" I wonder what you meant?'

'Please will you make me a chimney brush?' she shouted. 'Don't you realise how much it hurts to have to depend on other people?'

'Say that again,' I countered, furious.

'Go to hell. I'll get Anthony to make me one.'

Anthony Swift was the good neighbour from two doors away who had got us out of many a pickle in the past.

'Got it! So when you say having to depend on other people you don't mean any other person, you mean me.'

'Yes, if you like! You! That old story! Having to depend on you! Is that what you want me to say?'

The Christmas showcase at which 'Chimney Sweeps Are Us' was premiered included junior classes in which semi-obese girls rolled around the floor in what I suppose was called Modern Dance; and an exhibition of ballroom dancing by a moon-faced lad and his impossibly beautiful partner. They had medals. The Sweeps stole the show. When they tapped their way to a wheel, Liz raced another woman to the newly forming line and elbowed her out of the way, grim of face and with downturned lips. I had talked her into wearing an unbuttoned flat cap that settled gently over her ears and then her eyes. The head fell off the brush I had made her.

'I've gone as far as I can go with this lot,' she said, bitterly. 'Either I do it properly or I don't do it at all.'

'That's you all over,' I said, intending encouragement.

'Oh, will you please shut up!' she shouted.

Eight years earlier, we had come as close as we ever did to breaking up over rows like this. Liz's solitary habits were beginning to oppress me and I found it difficult to control the exasperation I felt. The proximate cause was the withering of anything spontaneous about us. My son Peter had come home from Princeton to teach at the university. Liz liked him. His brand of airy nonsense, fuelled by best bitter, could be tolerated because it went along with awesome intelligence. The anecdotes that derived from the people he drank with in city-centre pubs and the altercations he took part in on homeward-bound buses, in supermarket queues and seminar rooms, were funny enough, but they disguised a contradictory need in him. For all the flimflam he was at heart private and inward. In this respect, Liz saw something in him that until now I had not.

In the short term, his return to England changed the game. Clare was in Germany, Steve in Sussex, but here in Oxford was a comprehensive schoolboy who had parlayed his way to becoming a don, without once abandoning a jot of who he was as a child. The great gift Peter had was to be himself, unmoderated. So far as one could tell, he regretted nothing, omitted nothing. He came home to two unhappy people.

'You can't ask someone to be taller,' he explained breezily. 'Grasp that and you grasp the root of the problem.'

We were marching in a rut. I felt I was being consigned to the role Liz had devised for her former husband, which was to be a necessary but clumsy adjunct to her real (yet hidden) self. The petty quarrels multiplied. She liked to go to the supermarket every afternoon, simply to walk around the aisles, thinking. She seldom bought anything, or if she did, came home with something like a bag of pears or a new notebook. Had the supermarket been local – and there were two to choose from – it might have been a different matter. But only Tesco's would do for these wanderings. It meant a two-mile dash down the busy ring road and I spent the time she was away trying to blank out images of road traffic accidents, death and disaster.

'The roads are there to be used.'

'But not everybody on them is scrabbling to find the Thomas Tallis CD or tuning out Radio Oxford. Or is the whole thing an exercise in tuning out?'

'I go there to gather my thoughts, yes.'

'I am working my socks off to keep up a house – our house – where you can gather your thoughts.'

'It's just something I do. I'm sorry if it annoys you but I'm not going to be told how to live my life. I am not some badly trained dog.'

'Why not save the petrol and move your stuff down to Tesco's and live there permanently?'

'Yes! If it would save this endless bickering we've fallen into.'

The rows moved to the bedroom. After a particularly childish argument about the distribution of the duvet and the number of pillows she needed to surround herself, like a corpse in a shallow grave, I moved into the back room – and stayed there for the rest of our time together. Now there were two areas in the house that I thought of as being out of bounds. The other was her office.

'I've always believed that in the end I might have to choose between work and you. I hoped I wouldn't have to,' she wrote in her secret notebook for that year, adding '[I'm] remembering a multitude of good things which would seem diminished if it finished.'

As it almost did. There's no doubt I behaved badly – very badly – and the dismay she felt at that was shaming. What seemed to have happened was that an impulsive and disordered man who talked too much had thrown in his lot with a mute. What made it worse was that talking about our problems – when we did – was an exercise in icy civility. No crockery was thrown, no kitchen knives flourished. We were characters in an Elizabeth North novel. She felt betrayed – and so did I. For four months things hung in the balance.

'What I thought you wanted,' she scribbled at the edge of one page of her journal, 'was no hassle and no unnecessary housewifely routines' – this last phrase one to baffle (or delight) m'learned friends. That she never said this to me directly, and indeed conducted her entire defence between the covers of a spiral-bound notebook never to be seen in her lifetime, was all part of the same problem. It seemed that it was not she who was being managed but me – the fictional Nina had found yet another weak and foolish man she must deal with by weary accommodation.

I cannot feel indignant about this: it was almost certainly my fault that I had disturbed her wish to be left alone, often with enough buffooneries to make stones weep and angels grind their teeth. What hurt was not that it happened but that what we had to complain about and how we tried to reconcile our differences made us both seem very shallow and inadequate people.

'I hate quarrelling,' she said one night, tears running down her cheeks.

But of course I had been raised in a house where there was nothing but quarrels. It was the poison in my blood. What I thought I had found with Liz was a relationship far, far away from the days of my childhood, and an antidote to all that was choked and half-realised in my previous life. But who you are is not a collection of suit-cases to be burned by the side of the road or flung from the stern of a ship. I was inalterable, just as she was.

For some of the time this disjunction took place, I was filming in Senegal. One afternoon we stopped the crew bus to talk to some women huddled in a field of stubble, not sitting down, not standing up, but haunched as if ready to flee. I asked everyone to donate to them the chocolate, biscuits and bottled water we had. A young girl hung about at the edge of things. She had a child on her back, tied to her by a cotton sling. The baby had malarial encephalitis, her head so huge it was difficult to look at without pity and terror. This was a child doomed to die within a week or month. Her mother smiled, holding a horribly white biscuit and half a bottle of lukewarm

Evian in her dusty hand. That smile – and the ugly and formless brown field in which we all stood – has returned to haunt me ever since. Liz and I were both writers, both in a modest way intellectuals and, it dawned on me, equally selfish and self-absorbed.

Maybe France had been the antidote to such despair, for both of us. As happens with people who decide to stay together and stick it out, the obvious wounds healed and the scars they left were more or less forgotten. I was fifty-five when all this bickering reached its climax and when it was over forced to face a very unpleasant fact. I could never change from the person I had always been – needy, impulsive, reckless and unreliable. Nor could Liz become other than she was. We remained a couple not because of who we were but in spite of that.

The road we lived in was given over to doing the right thing, as described in the pages of the broadsheet papers. Most of us thought left, or leftish; most of us were pro-European and anti-American. We were a small colony of graduates and professionals devoted to the idea of appropriate behaviour. It was true that we ourselves happened to live next door to the only house that was rented out to students from hell, just as we were the only householders who did not need to get up early and commute to London or elsewhere. Simply put, we were, in the eyes of others, old folks. It had its attractions.

'I don't know whether you drink a lot of wine at home,' someone said at a party, detaching herself from her husband to make a little polite conversation.

'We do what we can,' Liz replied.

'Well, we just adore Cahors. We go to the place itself every year just to drink it at source.'

'How adventurous people are these days. Do you speak French?'

'The children are learning it at school. Emily is having a plunge at German.'

Ah, yes, the children. Many of the parents had put themselves in the position of being akin to racehorse trainers, cosseting their children towards the equivalent of the Derby Stakes – university and then a job in front of the cameras as foreign correspondents or arts-based documentary makers, MPs, novelists, the composers of rock operas, superstars.

'We took Charlie to Vienna last month,' this woman said, 'to give him an overview of the Secessionists. He was thinking about becoming a doctor and joining Médecins sans Frontières. But you see his girlfriend (who's very sweet) is arty. He mumbles a lot but I think he's a bit smitten by *la vie Bohème*.'

Followed by semi-hysterical laughter.

The Mrs Weldon book was published in the year 2000 to warm and generous reviews. Arabella commissioned a new book on the intertwined lives of some other strikingly eccentric figures, perhaps the most notable of them General Gordon of Khartoum. (I particularly relished the story of his decommission from the Chinese Army he had so successfully commanded. Grateful Shanghai merchants presented him with, among other things, a Western-style suit of exquisite cloth and cut. He had it towed behind a paddle steamer down filthy irrigation canals, the better to indicate how little material possessions mattered. The parcel that bobbed about in the wake of the steamer included a brand new bowler hat.)

Such spectacular renunciation of fame and fortune was Gordon's trademark. When he was sent to Egypt to resolve the war between HMG and the Mahdi, there was a telling scene enacted at the railway station. At the very last minute someone had the wit to ask him if he was well supplied with money for the journey. He had no money on him at all and those present had to empty their pocketbooks to help him on his way. There is an element of calculation in this and many of the more quixotic episodes in his life. He needed to advertise his superiority over the common man, even if that man was the Foreign Secretary. The source of his moral superiority was his utter indifference to what people thought of him.

I wrote the book, which was published as *Imperial Vanities* in 2001, in the shadow of Liz's own understanding of men. So very few were worth the candle, so very many self-deceiving. If her novel *Dames* was to believed, the test of a good man was his kindness, something of which only a woman could be the judge. By that measure, *Imperial Vanities* was for her a long gallery of rogues and charlatans, married to some notably intelligent and sensitive women.

All except Gordon, for whom celibacy was second nature. No man or woman could temper his disdain of others or moderate his monastic attempts at self-annihilation. His mother and his sister were conventionally devout but he was something far beyond even their understanding. There was the puzzle. In Liz's eyes, Gordon was, whatever his military triumphs, a negligible figure. Yet when he was stabbed to death on the stairs of the Governor's Residence in Khartoum, the hysteria surrounding his passing carried all the way to the throne. I wrote the last paragraphs of this book with Liz very much in mind.

The queen was at Osborne when she received the news. It was morning and she walked unaccompanied to the cottage occupied by the family of her private secretary. Lady Mary Ponsonby was still at breakfast with her two daughters when Victoria walked in and stood at the doorway, a short stout woman in her sixties whose expression had grown more sour with every year of her reign. Lady Ponsonby scraped back her chair, terrified. The queen stared at her for a few moments and then said, without preamble, 'Khartoum has fallen. Gordon is dead' . . . [She] inclined her head to Lady Ponsonby's few semi-coherent remarks and then left, trudging back to the house, where the tall windows reflected an image of herself, a little black-clad old lady barely taller than a child, Queen of England and Empress of India.

'Unbelievable,' Liz said softly when she read these sentences.

'You think it's too glib?'

'That degree of veneration is completely incomprehensible to me. Tell me about Lady Ponsonby.'

'She was very spiritually minded. Beautiful, strong-willed. She loved her husband and understood him. He had to put up with some awful nonsense from Victoria. It killed him in the end. Why do you ask?'

'I was trying to imagine what she was thinking when Victoria burst in. It's the idea of them being at breakfast that does it, somehow. It's the bit I shall always remember about the book.'

'Nothing else?'

'Oh, it's all wonderful of course. Upsetting. But wonderful. It stinks of men. What a to-do it all was.'

And glanced at her watch before trudging back upstairs. We had scraped together enough money to have the loft converted, in which her office was now located.

15

The Dinner Gong

Liz was seventy in 2002. Her style was settled and though she spent a lot of time protecting the image she had finally adopted (by choosing wisely and never buying on impulse) she felt no need to defend how she looked. The glamorous and ambitious Tania cut her hair, which she ruffled the moment she left the salon. She was not the sort of granny to wear skirts or blazers and though her jeans and a succession of faded pink baseball caps raised a few eyebrows, her look – as they say in the fashion magazines – was all of a piece. Her cheeks were lined but unpowdered, she wore no lipstick and affected very little jewellery, other than a penchant for necklaces worn as a form of mayoral chains. At parties, she fidgeted in boxy little jackets and ankle-length skirts. She was, as she explained to people who complimented her, making an effort.

Long before she opened her mouth to speak, she was perceived as a class act. She once invited a twenty-year-old student to lunch one snowy day in Oxford. The two had never met face to face. This girl rang me up and said that though she was there at the appointed time, there was no sign of Liz. In the background I could hear traffic passing.

'Go inside, look for a classy broad with a glass of Muscadet in her hand. That's your date.'

'A very intelligent girl,' Liz commented when she got home. 'She walked straight up to me, shook my hand and said "Hello, Liz". I could have been anybody.'

A coterie of highly intelligent women began to gather round her. They in turn were stylish and eye-catching, whose histories had left them quizzical, wide-awake, and (I choose the adjective carefully) undefeated. Two of them, Wendy and Evelyn, joined her in searching out church hall venues and laying on what they called bops – dancing to seventies music until the back suddenly gave out or the knees refused. Men were not barred from these gigs but neither were they begged to be there.

We made particular friends with Wendy, another rueful public schoolgirl with a beguiling CV as a career journalist, but one which included a spell as a bus driver and – latterly – any amount of voluntary work with alcoholics and drug users. Wendy did good in the world – not because she was called to it by a higher power but because what was wrong with society was right there under her nose. She read poetry to the blind, taught illiterate ex-prisoners and primary school children to read and write, washed up dirty crocks at one night refuge, made sandwiches at another, all without an ounce of piety. Some of her stories were truly hair-raising. We met once a week and these evenings descended through high-minded discussions about social theory to recent anecdotes about family life, and so, inevitably, to roars of laughter.

It may be that Liz had finally found the safe haven she had left resolutely unexplored. That things had not always turned out well in the past was no surprise to her: she was honest enough – and gifted enough – to see that the road she had chosen was by its nature rocky and occasionally desolate. Her literary reputation depended upon the mordancy of her wit, which never left her, but which she could no longer apply to the written word. By now there were twenty or more quarto notebooks tucked away in her office that no one had ever seen. Some of the contents were in effect field notes to the journey she had taken – feelings she had dissembled, misdirections given in the name of love, dismay at the reaction of others. She was never slothful, never bored. The silence in which she spent the working part of the day was given over to thinking. Increasingly, the tone of the notes she made became spiritual.

She joined a small group created by Shirley Harriot to examine the correspondences between Christianity and Hinduism. For her it was a way of exploring the contemplative aspects of religion, something she found missing in church-going. The study group she joined was an intellectual exercise that in the strict sense had no conclusion. It was for her a necessary form of rigour. At the same time, she was an old-fashioned Christian with a deep loyalty to ritual. In France, she would excuse herself from shopping or sightseeing to enter some cool and silent church to light candles in remembrance of the dead. A church was, after all, a place to be serious in. So it was with the Shirley Harriot group.

'I have been put in charge of the gong,' she said with quiet pride one evening. When she came home from the next meeting, I asked her how the gong work was going.

'I have had it taken away. It's a very small gong, probably a dinner gong and when the time came to sound it, I missed completely and hit the woodwork it was hanging from. Which of course was considered more than just bad luck.'

From the very beginning, the most telling thing about all the notebooks she filled is that only very, very seldom is anyone close to her mentioned by name. They were not a diary. As a mother and grandmother, she found it better to be the woman that by convention she was supposed to be. Her grandchildren found her kind and generous and unfailingly welcoming. Waiting for a visit from them, she would hear the knock at the door, close up her current notebook and come downstairs happy. This tenderness, which was wonderful to observe, extended to our own relationship. Both in appearance and in fact, we had come through.

One of her children lived in Cornwall and there is a photograph Jo took of her mother under the canopy of the up-line at St Erth when she was on her way back to Oxford. The train from Penzance that she had planned to take has just hurtled past without stopping. Liz stands with her hands in her jeans pockets, her travel bag and another from the Tate St Ives gift shop over her forearm, looking wonderfully serene and unruffled. There is no one else on the platform and the diffused light that filters through the canopy shows a handsome woman at peace with the world. It is the person I always look for walking towards me down a crowded Cornmarket in Oxford, or perhaps magically revealed in Holland Park Avenue, sipping a tisane at a pavement café and nibbling at the *Spectator* crossword.

There is a second memorable photograph of her sitting next to Deb Gill at High Table in Trinity Great Hall. The occasion was the wedding of Deb's daughter Caroline. The two lifelong friends are sitting side by side, each holding a glass of white wine with an identical pose, their planted elbows and loosely held hands around the stem of the wineglass like mirror images. Deb is looking affectionately at her chum: Liz leans forward and gazes out at the hundred or so wedding guests below her, the beginnings of a rueful smile on her face. Neither is the slightest bit fazed by the surroundings.

I could not say the same myself. I had not been back to Cambridge since 1958 and drove about looking for fingerposts to the past. What I remembered as a city of cyclists and gowns had been swept aside by the car. Liz had booked the overnight accommodation and the first great shock of the weekend had been when she rummaged in her bag and announced we were staying in Perne Road, where much of my childhood was spent.

To say that it was coarsened was to understate the case. One of the features when I lived there was the generous grass verges that many residents voluntarily mowed to a cricket-pitch closeness. In our time there, we were considered the only problem family in a street of clerks who knew their place. Either I had gone up in the world or Perne Road had struck a reef and sunk. Now these same verges were rutted with the wheeltracks of parked cars and vans. The houses, the whole neighbourhood, which my father had always advised us was better than we deserved, seemed small and shabby. The pavements and front gardens (where these still existed) pullulated with children; riding bikes about to be sure, but only in the manner of circus entertainers. I tried to remember how many children I knew in my own time there. The answer was five.

'We could go and find your house,' Liz suggested.

The idea filled me with dread. The place we were staying at was a bed and breakfast run by Greeks. They were friendly and unassuming and the husband clearly had a second income as some sort of small trader. The front room was stacked with boxes: this was a house where the man was king. We sat in the bedroom drinking tea, listening to the children rampage up and down. The window looked out onto other houses. I remembered that once there had been wheatfields and the path to a cement works. Practically as much as I knew about the countryside had been located outside this window, where now there were washing carousels and barbeque trolleys, pink plastic tricycles and garden sheds.

There was something very unsettling about all this, from the ruination of what I remembered about the locality and the people who lived there then to the person I had become, travelling in morning dress to a wedding in Trinity. The cab let us off in King's Parade and we walked the rest of the way through clouds of tourists. Liz held my hand.

'I'm really sorry,' she said. 'I didn't realise what I was doing when I booked the place.'

'Just don't let me leave this top hat anywhere.'

'Shouldn't you be wearing it?'

I was too shaky to answer.

After the wedding service, which was held in Trinity Chapel, I was walking across Great Court with an elderly woman who asked me in that false drawl the comfortably-off affect, 'Were you lucky enough to go to University?'

'As it happens, I was a member of this very college.'

She was not disposed to believe me; or maybe I was looking for insult where there was none. She chewed on things for a moment or two, smoothing the skirt to her silk suit as we walked. She was exactly the kind of woman Liz was supposed to be, *soignée*, not very intelligent, but capable of a banality that could fell elephants.

'How amazing it must have been, to be in the company of so many intelligent people.'

'To be perfectly honest, I was so bloody intelligent myself I barely noticed anyone else.'

Talking to her – better to say encouraging her first impression of me as a very rude and unpleasant person – I was thinking instead of Perne Road, where the most sophisticated person I knew when I lived there as a child was a trainee reporter on the *Cambridge Daily News*. He wore a black beret and was always dressed in the same Fair Isle pullover, topped by a ridiculous yellow bow tie. I could remember his long fingers and the affectation he had of using them to roll matchstick thin cigarettes which he smoked with a theatrical flourish. But the most memorable thing about him was that his parents adored him.

'You look as though you have seen a ghost,' Deb smiled.

'Do you think I'm any good?' I asked.

'What a question. Whizz loves you, so I should think you're amazing. Well, she's said as much, as lately as ten minutes ago.'

'Maybe she was talking about my hair.'

Deb laughed her rich honey chuckle. Just before the

wedding, I had gone to Tania and persuaded her to dye my hair white, for I was to represent the bride's father at the wedding feast, and there is nothing more nerve-wracking. The requirement was to be jocular in just the right way. Part of my speech was already going round in my head like a carousel pony. I proposed to say that in my time as an undergraduate I had spent many hours discussing girls and how to get them. Just about the last thing I could have imagined was that here, today, I was giving one away.

Earlier I had shown Liz the huge chestnut tree that dominates New Court, in which I had often roosted, after a night spent drinking something called Yugoslav Riesling, which was probably employed in its country of origin as drain cleaner.

'Were you alone?'

'More often than not. Do people still climb this tree?' I asked a passing student.

He cocked his head and studied me politely. 'Um, why would they want to do that?'

'It does seem a bit out of the ordinary,' Liz commented.

'I was there in search of my inner child,' I said.

'You once told me you were naked, more often than not.'

'That does take some explaining, yes.'

Now, with the coat to my rented morning dress draped around Deb's shoulders to shield her from a Fen breeze, I was sitting – I was sprawling – on the lawns of Neville's Court with a hundred others, where once no foot had trod, save for a Fellow of the College who had taken it on himself to mow the sacred grass to a nicety. He was always accompanied by the Head Porter, there to give official sanction. I felt depressed and antsy. I was as much a stranger here as I had been in Perne Road – or indeed up the chestnut tree in the adjacent court.

'Is Michael Challis here?' I asked suddenly.

The very first Englishman we met in France was someone who was recommended to us by Deb. He came to the house when it was more Gaston's than ours. We ate outdoors, in company with Paul and Callie, and a squadron of bats, and though the meal was nothing very much, it was attacked by this man with almost animal ferocity. It was night and the scene was lit by a single hurricane lamp, against which green insects from the maize fields hurled themselves. Yes, he knew Deb, he said, licking his plate clean; and yes, he came from Oxford. At this moment he was living in a house not unlike our own where there was trouble with marauding frogs. They attacked at night. His French neighbours, such as he had, were gloomy and suspicious folk. Maybe they saw that he was not entirely comfortable with mere tittle-tattle, he added, a remark I put down to artistic temperament.

There was a reason for this misunderstanding. Liz had invited him as someone Deb knew well, a sculptor I might like to meet. I had anticipated a bearded giant with blunt nails and a denim smock. He was in fact small and neat, wearing a striped shirt with the sleeves buttoned down. By speech and gesture he resembled a pencil-pusher much more than a man who wrestled with sculptural form. But I paid him the respect due to a master. When I was suffi- ciently drunk, I broached the idea of becoming his pupil.

'For a fee?'

'Yes, for a fee. I want to learn how to carve in wood.'

'What sort of thing?'

'Nudes, I imagine,' Callie supplied with a sly smile.

'I'm afraid somewhere along the line we have got our wires crossed. I am not a sculptor. I am a physicist. I am also extremely unhappy.'

Liz was at a loss to explain this surreal evening, with bats skimming overhead and the oppressive silence of the maize fields pressing down. We never saw our guest again. He had simply swum up from some froggy swamp for one night only and then driven back there in a battered 2CV.

'Perhaps he really was a sculptor and invented all the rest to keep us at bay,' she suggested.

'The bit about being unhappy rang true, though.'

'Yes,' she murmured. 'That much was pretty obvious.'

'No mention of wives or girlfriend, did you notice?'

'I think Deb might have mentioned some problems in that area.'

'Although she could have been thinking of somebody else.'

'That can happen with Deb, yes.'

In this way we fluffed our sole meeting with the distinguished author, physicist and investigator into the notion of time, Michael Challis. It is no great surprise that he never returned the hospitality: he must have thought us barking mad. He had come to Charente to sit in a chair and think, watched by a chorus of frogs to be sure, but described by a single preoccupation. By comparison, my mind was just so much shovelled sand.

We were on more solid ground with the incomparable Dick and Daphne Mayne. Dick was a retired Captain RN and Daphne his wonderfully sardonic consort. They lived up on the ridge where Kath and Trev were renovating their *auberge*. Daphne was thin, in the elegant way of things, smoked with an actor's dash, and favoured gin in wardroom measures. She was an anecdotalist of genius.

'One year, I was coming home from Bombay while Dick was piking off somewhere with his flotilla, and my dear! The people on that boat! I had the squidgepots with me, of course, and after three days this ghastly woman came up and asked "Do your children play Scrabble?" And I said, understandably enough, "How the *hell* would I know?"'

She knew Kath and Trev by sight. Two more badly assorted neighbours could hardly have been found in all Christendom.

'We met briefly in the Rouillac surgery one morning. My dear! She was exactly the sort of person one finds in a waiting room. She wanted to talk to me about her knees. Her husband was engrossed, I mean absolutely engrossed, in a plumber's catalogue. I believe they are fossicking about with the house on the main road. Haunted of course.'

'Do you think so?'

'So the locals say. But then we lived in a house in Hampshire said to be haunted. Dick was all for the place but quite omitted to mention that a river ran through the sitting room.'

'Underneath the floor, darling,' Dick protested mildly. He turned to us. 'It was an old mill, d'you see? Picturesque, but easy to rent.'

'Because of the noise from the bloody river.'

'Culvert is a better description. It could be vexing,' he allowed, with a sort of Christopher Isherwood smile.

'You say it was haunted.'

'May have been. Was once, perhaps. What remaining ghosts there were left soon after Daphne arrived. Scooted, you might say.'

'Bested,' she said, pouring us all the first drink of the day.

They lived in a modern architect-designed house, with a separate bungalow for guests. Their swimming pool was there to be used. Liz and she paddled up and down chatting about children, she in a preposterous white bathing cap from the fifties and a floral swimsuit that hung on her freckled shoulders like a sitting-room curtain. Dick and I sat in the shade, drinking single malts in companionable silence. He was a very good-looking man with tremendous manners. Most of his time in the navy had been spent at sea, all served in stations that required his particular brand of diplomacy. He and Daphne were devoted to each other: his contribution to the relationship was that same easy and undemanding charm.

'We were in Bahrain when they sent out this amazing Admiral whose father was a painter of some kind,' Daphne began when the drinks were refreshed.

'Casper John,' Liz suggested.

'Indeed. Did you know him?'

'I knew of him. He and Dylan Thomas's future wife were childhood sweethearts.'

'Good God! Anyway, I was placed next to him at lunch and I could see things were going to be sticky from the start. Do you shoot? I asked. No. Well, do you hunt? No. Ah well, so you fish. No. And so I looked him straight in the eye and said "Look here, you bloody man, I am trying to make conversation."'

'Verbatim,' Dick confirmed. 'He was of course First Sea Lord at the time.'

Daphne had found her audience with us. When Dick went into hospital ('to be rodded out, as far as I can grasp the procedure,' he explained ruefully) she came down the hill for drinks, always with a monologue of sobbingly funny stories – about Admirals and ratings, British Consuls and what she called the local natives. Like Liz, she had been born to a class that had been overwhelmed by events.

'It comes to something when a grocer's daughter is the acme of political wisdom. The Queen, poor woman, detests her.'

'Is there a woman you would have accepted as Prime Minister?'

'Oh, Elizabeth David without a doubt. Hands down, every time. But it's a bit late for that.'

'I remember how people used to give copies of her books as wedding presents.'

'In Germany they gave *Mein Kampf*. The author insisted on it. My dear, can you imagine the thrill of reading in bed together in those happy days? One can imagine even the most frigid frau turning to sex in desperation.'

'What do you read, Daphne?'

'James Michener. I like to see people paint with a broad brush.'

She often stayed until one in the morning, driving away with total sang froid, sometimes with her lights on, sometimes not.

'I've had such a lovely evening,' she would croon, before buzzing off into the night like a speeding ambulance.

*   *   *

Perhaps we knew too many people whose histories were like flies trapped in amber. Twentieth-century politics had a poor record for carrying the old along with it. What had been was by definition redundant. This is not the same thing as describing those politics as progressive. What I think happened was that little by little the time horizons contracted, so that what lay in the past was abandoned as being irrelevant and the future was so badly described that it hardly encompassed next weekend. Liz once took a grandchild to London and asked her who she supposed the statue of Churchill in Parliament Square represented. Jenny, an intelligent and buzzy teenager, thought it might possibly be a record producer, though she could not say which one. In France I showed a boy a war memorial across from the café where he sat glugging Coca-Cola. I asked him what it could be. He suggested it had something to do with horse racing.

Liz was born thirteen years after the first transatlantic flight by Alcock and Brown (in an adapted First World War bomber) and four years after the first east–west flight by Koehl and Fitzmaurice. Imperial Airways was in existence as the sole British carrier on international routes but even its most prestigious planes carried no more than twenty people. When she was four years old, the defence budget was increased in response to the German menace to provide for a further 250 planes. By the time she was eight, in 1940, nearly three thousand aircraft were produced in the last quarter of that year alone. Spitfires were being manufactured at the rate of a hundred a week.

The statistics do not tell the story. What makes the story is the image of her watching the Portsmouth Blitz from her bedroom window; later, cycling down Hampshire lanes in search of Americans to give her gum and Hershey bars and finding to her amazement they had all vanished, leaving behind empty barbed wire enclosures and muddy wheel tracks reflecting back the June skies. One of the planes flying over her head that D-day had my father in it, an hour or so later being bounced about in flak, his navigator table ripped to pieces.

The war and its aftermath were the great milestones in both our lives. We were children with something to remember and perhaps it was natural to look for other people with long memories. In any case, the old huddle together. They get in the way of the young and clutter up the buses, the NHS waiting lists, the middle lanes of motorways and airport queues. They infest radio phone-ins with their reactionary nonsense and given half a chance at neighbourhood parties ramble on about films like *In Which We Serve* or *This Happy Breed*. Their obituaries, when they come, are signals from a past that might as well be from outer space. After all, who *was* Churchill and who cares about old-time stuff like war memorials?

The French date their Victory Day from the liberation of Paris and de Gaulle's speech from the balcony of the Hôtel de Ville. Every year, a minister of the government with special regard for *les anciens combattants*, sends to every commune in France a single sheet of paper requiring the population to present itself at war memorials in order to honour the dead. In Bresdon, this takes place at the communal cemetery and is attended by some hundred or more citizens. Many of those present were young children when the Germans held the country but there are others who cannot remember the war and are present to celebrate what de Gaulle called in his speech 'eternal

France'. Only those who are thirty or under are missing. They are conspicuous by their absence. A rock concert, a dash to the coast, maybe only a morning in bed with one's lover has intervened. First things first. We cannot remember what we never had.

16

Keeping Mum

The last of the most ambitious books I wrote was *Devastating Eden*, published in 2004. It was a double biography of the nineteenth-century mill owner and would-be social reformer, Robert Owen and his intellectual opposite, a Württemberg vine-dresser, George Rapp. They were connected by a place – a frontier town called Harmony on the Wabash River – and a dangerous idea. Each of these ill-assorted men was in the broadest sense utopian. In the ordinary course of history, it was almost inconceivable they should ever meet.

The hedge-priest Rapp had come to America with 1,300 of his followers in search of a place to wait out the harrowing of the world foretold in the Book of Revelations. Only the most devout would be spared, to live out the last thousand years of human existence in peace and harmony before God extinguished His entire creation. But first the world as it was at present must be renounced. Somewhere in the wilderness (but who knew where?) the scriptural Woman Clothed in the Sun was waiting for the Rappites. They might have chosen Russia to search for her but what was called at the time 'Amerika-fever' drew them across the Atlantic. It was this semi-ecstatic search for salvation in what was still a sparsely populated land mass that Rapp promised his followers. The essence of this millenarian vision was that it could not be contradicted. Armageddon was fact.

Owen, coming from the polar opposite to this belief, held that he alone, by the application of reason, had discovered a way to change human nature and bring into being a new moral order. All other authority was superseded. Everywhere he looked Owen found error, mountains of it. So it had been in the New Lanark Mills he bought from his father-in-law. He turned his investment into a showcase of enlightened man-management and commercial profitability by altering what he called 'the human machinery' – that is to say the drunken and recalcitrant mill hands. Self-taught, stubborn, icily indifferent to human vagary, Owen had no religious belief whatever. All that was required of his workforce was that it should do exactly as it was told. The same went for society at large. What he had done for a single cotton mill, he could do for all mankind.

In one sense, the story of the book was simplicity itself. In 1824, Owen bought Rapp's frontier town Harmony lock, stock and barrel. It bankrupted him and the new moral order on which his hopes were based collapsed into farce and ignominy. He had failed to notice – or if he had, discounted the fact – that the undeniable prosperity of Harmony, hacked into existence from among the tall timbers, depended on the free labour of Rapp's adherents. There was a high-minded Harmony Society that excited the admiration of liberals and democrats;

but some innocent-looking clauses to the constitution might have merited Owen's closer scrutiny.

Rapp – or Father as the devout called him – had made one fortune from the Harmony Society and with its sale went on to accumulate another. Under his direction, men and women slept in separate dormitories and only met each other to pray and be harangued by Father at weekends. Marriage among the faithful was discouraged to the point that it was practically unheard of. No outsiders were permitted to join the Society: people who absconded were vilified in lengthy Sunday anathemas. (If they could be traced, they were hunted down and beaten half to death.) It was true of Rapp's Harmony that theoretically all goods were held in common, as commended in the Bible, but when it came to actual specie, the dollars earned from some very aggressive trading were kept in a deep coffer under Father's bed.

Owen seemed not to have realised that Harmony was a slave camp in all but name. The slaves were willing enough – they were, after all, driven by prophecy – but no more distinguishable one from another than were ants. They had no opinion about their condition and were completely incurious about their host country. They spoke German to each other, prayed in German, and when they went out into the fields sang the old hymns of their childhood. A town band, said to be the first in America, accompanied them.

The only way Owen could replicate Harmony's commercial success was to call on the resources of what had begun to be called Owenism. He advertised for right-minded people to join him and embrace the principles he had devised. There was an egalitarian tinge to his prospectus, too, but in reality those who came to the New Harmony had to accept that Owen alone had the power and the means to reconstruct their nature in the way the project required. The town was a commercial proposition, but much, much more a laboratory for the extinguishing of baneful error. He had sunk his entire personal wealth into the first and all his crack-brained ideas into the second.

The project instantly attracted freeloaders, contrarians, charlatans and a fair cross-section of the socially useless, including many who had never worked with their hands. Cabbages rotted in the fields because it was beneath the dignity of anyone to cut them. Pigs rooted up the little cottage gardens Rapp's loyal subjects had planted. The New Harmonists turned out to be incorrigible. Something for nothing – better still, pennies from heaven – was what had drawn them to Indiana. Meanwhile, no amount of moral persuasion could touch them. It was the California gold rush without the gold. Owen had hired a rabble.

I wrote this book in some part out of dismay. It was published three years after British troops were committed to Afghanistan, sent there by a Secretary of State who believed they would hardly be called upon to fire a shot, so powerful was the wonder drug they brought with them – America's version of democracy. As in the Owenite model of human society, all that was required to render the country peaceful was for those who lived in Afghanistan to give up the ancient error of their ways. Their medieval brand of religiosity, about which they were so stubborn, was a token of how steeply they had fallen behind the curve.

In 1855, a much chastened Robert Owen convened a meeting in Long Acre, London, which he advertised with trademark vanity as The World's Convention of Delegates from the Human Race. Owen had only three years to live and he was there to unveil The Universal Peacemaker, not a moral argument but a machine, as yet unbuilt. The Devastator, as it was swiftly dubbed, would be capable of producing such awesome and remorseless firepower that in ten hours it would deliver up a million souls to their Maker. In ten days, the Devastator would end the war on terror for all time. If the unregenerate mass of the human race could not be persuaded by reason to alter their nature, then annihilation would follow. In some way or other, after the smoke cleared, Owenism would remain intact and triumphant.

The epigraph to this book was taken from Rousseau's *Discourse on the Origin and Basis of Inequality Among Men*:

> If I were told that society is so constituted that each man gains by serving others, I should reply that that would be all very well but for the fact that he gains even more by harming them. No profit is so legitimate that it cannot be surpassed by what can be done illegitimately, and a harm done to a neighbour is always more lucrative than any good turn.

On the way home at the end of one summer, we were stuck in fog behind a tailback of cars that were hung up behind a tractor. Quite suddenly, the whole of the rear window was filled with the image of a white supermarket pantechnicon, driving more or less on our bumper. The young driver amused himself by honking and flashing his lights and when he'd had enough of that, overtook us and the whole tailback. He missed an oncoming car by inches, forcing the driver (a terrified old woman) nose-down into a ditch. The tractor fled into a field and at once all the French set off after the truck on full beam, their horns baying. Within a hundred yards, they were swallowed up in the fog.

'That was close,' Liz commented. 'Why did he do it?'

'For pride of life, maybe.'

'Or because he's seen too many GB plates lolloping along.'

'What's so hateful about us?'

'If you're young, pretty much everything, I should have thought.'

'We're too old?'

'Too decrepit.'

The remark lingered. After two more seasons of mobilette adventures out among the maize fields, which included a further visit to the A & E in Cognac (loose shale), Liz was surfeited. We spent a last season of gardening and reading, before deciding to sell the house in France. It was a huge wrench. We left behind unpayable debts of gratitude to our French neighbours. The only book I had in print in France was what they would call a *polaire* – a detective story.

Paulette Ayraud, to whom I had dedicated the work, was characteristically scolding.

'This sort of book you could write anywhere. Madame Elizabeth says you need a good library. We have a good library. It comes once a fortnight in a van driven by M. Berthier. So don't use that as an excuse. You've grown bored by us.'

194

'You don't really think that, Paulette.'

'Oh, we're very dull, we know that. Not to be compared with all your rich English friends.'

Later that day she came down with a bucket of courgettes as a peace offering. As a bonus, we got a short history of village delinquencies, from the man who had groped her as a teenager when she was doing nothing more alluring than forking manure, to more recent scandals, some of them extremely alarming.

'*Il était là, devant votre portaille, en pleine vue, jouant avec son piquet.*'

I could not imagine what pleasure a man could get playing with his fencepost.

'*Son piquet,*' Paulette corrected, jumping up and giving a very good imitation of a man masturbating. Liz fetched her notebook and copied out the other synonyms Paulette used for human genitalia. They included *canne-à-papa, carotte, cornemuse, macaron, manche, trombone, biscuit, thermomètre-à-moustaches, pain-au-lait, poisson rouge. . .*

'This is excellent!' Liz enthused.

Paulette examined our faces for irony and finding none, grinned. I had for a long time described her as the Queen Mother, a title she applied to herself with equal enthusiasm. 'I shall miss you both,' she said fondly, kissing Liz on the cheek.

One of the farewell explorations we made was to Rochefort, the last piece of French soil Napoleon trod before taking a boat out to the *Bellerophon* and there surrendering his sword to Captain Frederick Maitland, RN. It was the first step of the way to St Helena. As he left France for exile, he passed the arsenal and navy yard we had come to visit and was cheered by a small crowd, though it seems likely they saluted him more out of pity than loyalty to the Emperor he no longer was. A titan had fallen. When his longboat was grappled to the hull of the *Bellerophon*, one of his entourage ran up on deck to announce him. Maitland stayed studiously on his quarterdeck, forcing Napoleon to come aboard without the usual honours, a short fat man with a horrible green pallor and dull eyes.

It was to visit this town and fort that we had come to the coast. The French were building a full-scale replica of the eighteenth-century frigate *Hermione*. The original was built at Rochefort in just eleven months – itself a matter of wonder. She foundered thirteen years later at Le Croisic, at the mouth of the Loire, in the revolutionary year of 1792. She had been driven onto the rocks and smashed to pieces by heavy gales. Using as far as was possible the original tools and building techniques, the French had set themselves the task of replicating the vessel, not because she was specially famous but to honour the days when French frigates were the acme of naval construction and the envy of all sea-going nations. She was, never mind her inglorious end, part of the patrimony of France.

It was this word – *patrimonie* – that had attracted me. I had last heard it spoken, with the greatest possible irony, on the slave island of Gorée, off the coast of Senegal. There is no exact counterpart in the English concept of history – for example Oxford is very seldom held out as a demonstration of national identity. (We care more for sites of special scientific interest these days, perhaps. One of the more memorable bits of television documentary in recent years was the sight of archaeologists on their hands and knees, fingercombing a meadow for crested newts before being allowed to dig for a Roman villa.)

It was Sunday and maybe two thousand visitors had lost themselves in the vast grounds laid out by Vauban. The way to the dockyards was marked by a *grande allée* that ran between emerald green lawns. Down its whole length were pollarded trees of identical height and roundness. On the left was the *cordellerie*, where ropes had been made. Up ahead, the dry docks. The site included two museums, bookshops, a restaurant and a café. Not one piece of paper blew in the wind, not one child had come with a football to kick about on the lawns. There were no transistors playing, not so much as a raised voice. The people we passed were not naval historians but locals and their families. There was a gallery in the dry dock from which the bare bones of the *Hermione*'s hull could be examined by men who understood wood and the labour it took to fashion it. It was all magical. The holiday season had yet to end in Rochefort and further north in Les Sables-d'Olonne and ten miles away on the Île d'Oléron there was noise and animation enough. But here, it seemed to me, we were about something else.

'And what is that?' Liz asked. Though it was a warm day, the wind was brisk and she sat with my sweater round her shoulders. She looked pale.

'Are you all right?'

'I'm sad about selling the house, I suppose. And days like this. Slow French afternoons like this. You're right. There's something magical about the place.'

'Can you say what?'

'That was the question I asked you.'

I told her about going to Wells Cathedral one day in

the sixties and finding a family who had chosen to hold their picnic on the altar steps, complete with chequered tablecloth, blue plastic plates and thermos flasks on the altar itself. They were being badgered by outraged church wardens. Dad put the situation as he saw it.

'Listen, mate. We own these places. So sod off.'

'It's not just that the people here are better behaved. They are reaching out for some form of seriousness about their nationality we don't have, perhaps never had.'

She pushed her wineglass away.

'But then we've never had a genocide on our own soil. I can say with my hand on my heart that I miss England, if that's what you want to hear me say. I miss my family. But that's not why we're going. We have had some great times in France but I was never so romantically inclined as you. About this or anything else we've done together.'

'Well, well,' I said through gritted teeth, passing her the car keys.

'Don't make a face. It's not a very great surprise, surely?'

'That you're not so romantically inclined? It's common knowledge, I'm sure.'

I pushed back my chair and tried to walk about like a Frenchman for a half hour or so, one who boiled inwardly with rage and self-pity. Like a lot of quarrels between partners, this one borrowed from the location. The sun beat down, there was that late-afternoon ennui that happens in hot countries and we were the only two people speaking in English.

She was waiting for me in the bookshop.

'A few postcards for the grandchildren?'

'I bought these for you,' she said in a small voice, flinching when I made to embrace her. One of the cards

198

illustrated the flag codes of the French eighteenth-century navy.

'Is there one that says "I am falling astern of station"?'

'This one says, "Make all speed and rejoin the Fleet,"' she said, jabbing at random. 'Please.'

The very last time we had a chance to thank the Boucherie family, who had done so much for us, was when they invited us to a picnic along the banks of the Charente. We were not to provide anything ourselves but simply follow them to a favoured spot. We parked our cars and walked a couple of hundred metres. The river ran glassy green. Overhead was a canopy of perfectly still branches. The only movement came from the swifts skimming the surface of the water. Arlette Boucherie and her daughter-in-law Ghyslaine began preparing what was to turn out to be a five-plate lunch. Their husbands laid out eel lines, murmuring to each other in low and unexcited tones. After twenty minutes, there was an issue of cider, which Rene explained was the only thing for a picnic. We were in a Cartier-Bresson photograph.

'Well, we shall have to see who follows you,' Rene said, smiling. 'It goes without saying you will be missed, madame.'

'We have received nothing but kindness from you all.'

'It has been hard for us to picture you as anything more than retired people who could live where they liked. But of course we don't really know how you live in England.'

'It would be hard to find a day as beautiful as this in England.'

It was too pat a compliment. He thought about saying more, then shrugged. Loosening his belt, he lay down on his back and slept. Ghyslaine slept beside Jean-Yves, her arm flung across his chest. It was the most intimate we had ever seen either of them. What it indicated, I think, was that so far as the Boucheries were concerned, we had already gone.

Back in England – newly bereaved, as it were – I was sitting at the desk one rainy morning when I opened a new file and began the personal history that became *Keeping Mum*. Nobody had asked for it and I surprised myself by thinking about it at all. This was a piece of self-deception: I had thought about little else, off and on, my whole adult life, sometimes without even knowing it. It took the writing of the book to make me realise this. I deleted the first half a dozen pages as being just too miserabilist for words. Put another way, I was laughing too much to see straight. I watched Liz out in the garden, wearing my golf jacket and wielding a yellow-handled set of shears in among the shrubs. She blew me a brief kiss. I was not asking the reader to take my side, nor condemn the two unhappy people who happened to be my parents. But then, why *was* I writing it?

After a couple of weeks I realised I had almost total recall of things said and done and, perhaps more importantly in the end, the geography of streets and rooms in which they took place. I could, if I wished, go to live there. In fact, I had the unusual experience of pushing on a door and walking into a landscape that had not changed one whit since the 1940s. I found I could remember the exact weight and heft of the cutlery we had or the stale smell of the upstairs lavatory. I felt as if I had only to get up from the desk to find these things unchanged, waiting, in some part of the house I presently owned. There, in that remembered world, the huge lavender hedge in the front garden still sprawled onto the pavement, the kitchen still stank of rotting floorboards and soap flakes. As I went on, I realised the deeper question the book posed was never going to be about blame, or revenge – nor even memory. Was I, sixty years on, the same needy and uncertain child I had been then? Find him – and find myself.

I could not have written this book while my parents were still alive. What I was to them was undeniably the main part of the story. What compensations there were for being their unloved son were few. One of these was the local grammar school, which rescued me from actual ruination. That was not its remit: the people who taught me would have been hard put to imagine where I came from or what calamities awaited me when I got home. Their business was other. Slowly but surely I was being reeled in from the emotional swamp I inhabited. I was a bright spark who could conjugate French irregular verbs or find pleasure – confusion but pleasure – in Shakespeare. It was all that was required of me. For my mother it was a form of magic, as for example when she found out I was studying Latin, akin to her of going into the woods at night to practise voodoo. My father was simply and crudely jealous: I was being given opportunities denied to him.

'I see you are wearing poofs' shoes,' he said, pointing to my Hush Puppies. 'I suppose it will be lipstick and eyeshadow next.'

'I haven't found a shade I like.'

The greater passport to freedom was sex – better to say running around and falling in love with anyone that would give me a kind word. In this I was my mother's child. I came home from excursions to the river or the far corners of the recreation ground, emotionally exhausted by an hour or so of fumbling nonsense, just as my mother had done with hungry Americans outside cinemas or in the back of jeeps.

'You don't want to go knocking up one of these girls, else soon enough you'll be pushing a roll of lino home in the baby's pram,' my favourite uncle warned. I was confused by the remark. It had never, perhaps never would, get as far as that. Jessie, my aunt, understood my blushes.

'He's not sixteen yet,' she chided. 'It's just a bit of slap and tickle, I shouldn't wonder. And good luck to the both of them.'

'One of us has just give you really good advice,' Jim said, chortling.

All this while the rabbit they kept in place of a cat sat on the kitchen table, studying me with unblinking attention.

I had quite accidentally written a bestselling book and laid a ghost that had haunted me all my life. *Keeping Mum* received stunning reviews and went on to win literary prizes I had always considered well beyond my grasp. There was only one downside to all this. In a year I too would be seventy.

Gounod, as I had discovered when writing about the disastrous Mrs Weldon, was a vain fool of a man in his private life, but did say one memorable thing about growing old. It was not, he claimed, the tenant that aged, but the house. It met my situation exactly. I had gone to one award ceremony in a cheap second-hand dinner jacket, which I intended to set off with a black tie that was not entirely a black tie. The gents' outfitter I consulted listened sympathetically.

'I think it seldom serves to vary the colour of the tie, sir. Do you have a special reason for breaking with tradition?'

'I feel I am being misrepresented in a dinner jacket.'

'You wear one infrequently?'

'You are looking at an elderly man with a balding head and rounded shoulders. But inside that man is a boy of about fifteen. That's who you are talking to now. How old are you, deep down?'

'My mother always said I was born elderly. I see your dilemma, sir. But I would strongly counsel against a coloured tie. Nor a velvet one. Very much not a velvet one. The boy you mention is a private matter, I imagine.'

It was a caution that came too late. The boy I mentioned had controlled my whole life, as the pages of *Keeping Mum* revealed, for those who had eyes to see.

'It explains everything,' an old flame wrote to me on publication. She knew whereof she spoke.

17

The End Game

The end game is everything, I would often tell her. If she asked me what that was, I replied with this: it will be that moment when all the work and effort pays off and we draw the benefits of a long life together. It will be our consummation and the way we will be remembered by others. We have to be realistic here and recognise that such a thing as the end game cannot be planned and must announce itself by indirection. Perhaps it will come prefigured as cherry blossom or the fall of rose petals, perhaps as the last leaf to fall in autumn. However it is, we will recognise its arrival as a new and inalterable serenity which previously we have only experienced in snatches.

In my mind this transformation had nothing to do with money. Bank and building society accounts, credit cards and all the rest of it would become merely so much redundant background chatter. For us, the end game would be finally played out in a house stuffed with books and overlooking the sea. The immediate view from the sitting-room windows would be a walled garden with wonderfully stocked borders. Only when (by agreement) a gate was left open, wedged by a brick or two, would we glimpse the sea, a rectangle of shifting blues and greens representing the real world, where some ships swam and some sank.

'I'm sure it's very nice,' she said, whenever I mentioned it.

'No, but don't you think we deserve such a place, if only as punctuation? All the subordinate clauses will gradually have dried up, the verbs grown cleaner. The silences longer, memory sleeping in its basket like a dog. I'm not describing Alzheimer's, Elizabeth. I'm talking about the gift I want to make you.'

'A house by the sea?'

'Halfway up Ben Nevis if you prefer,' I said, nettled.

'It's the idea of the end game itself I'm jibbing at. It's very poetic but sounds a bit too much like la-la land to me. Won't we be surrounded by neighbours whom we hate, all of them the natural enemies of metaphor? People with healthy bank accounts and wonderful cars, private healthcare and all the rest of it. We are not just describing an exalted form of retirement plan here, are we?'

'We are not. How could we be? Neither of us will ever stop working, I know that. Nor will we change from who we are. I'm talking about getting what we deserve, in some form yet to declare itself.'

That Christmas, she discovered a lump under her arm. By the middle of January, after an operation to remove as many of her lymph nodes as surgical protocol allowed, she was diagnosed with cancer of unknown position. The end game had come to greet us.

The Churchill hospital was begun in 1940 to prepare for unknown numbers of casualties from the German bombing soon to be unleashed upon us. Churchill had widely predicted this onslaught, maybe as many as a million casualties in the first year of war. His wife Clementine gave her name to the humanitarian response. When these mass injuries did not materialise, the buildings were rededicated in 1942 to the care of US Army battle casualties. Part of the hospital is now the home of the Oxford Cancer Unit, a facility with an international reputation. Soldiers brought here in the war would not recognise the new buildings. In the last two decades, the Churchill has shed its higgledy-piggledy look and become a small architect-designed town.

One of the trials all cancer patients in the developed world have to suffer is well-meaning anecdotal evidence put forward by friends and relatives. Everybody knows someone whose brother-in-law's uncle was completely cured of the disease by eating liquidised grass or concentrated fish extracts, becoming a born-again Christian, or being given his own personal mantra to chant eight hours a day. The internet has done nothing to lessen this unintentioned cruelty. A sportsman in San Diego, a woman lawyer in Seattle, a drinks hostess in Las Vegas etc., etc. – all of them have some special story to tell of how they beat the odds. Round every patient's bedside, therefore, find a small knot of people unable to comprehend what has happened and hoping against hope for a way out of the mess.

The eerie calm of the Oncology Unit at the Churchill is their standing reproof. With great skill and compassion, patients are led to an understanding of what is happening to them. It is only terrifying because it is so unequivocal. Outside the sun is shining, reflected back in hundreds of windscreens, the football season has reached its critical few weeks. Who knows whether we will have a warm summer or our team will qualify for Europe – or face relegation? Will the Harrisons next door go bankrupt or Jack marry Jill? Will a change of government make things better or worse for the country? Shall we have salad tonight, or a bit of fish?

Inside the hospital, there is this carefully nurtured calm. Nobody runs, nobody screams, and after a week or two, nobody flinches. Visitors learn it is bad form – or perhaps bad juju – to ask after others. The lifts are powered by a horribly charged silence and shyly exchanged smiles. The NHS has directed friends and relatives not to bring flowers into the wards any longer. We follow each other along silent corridors in single file, the shadows we cast like bruises on the immaculate floors. The sunlight mocks us. If behind a half open staff door a nurse laughs at something an orderly has said, it strikes us all as cruel and uncaring, like laughter in church. We ourselves are treading extra carefully, as might communicants on their way to the altar rail.

Not everybody wanted Liz to have the four tranches of chemotherapy the unit wanted her to have. I talked her into it, holding her hands in mine. We had seen the PET scan that showed a dozen or more tiny green blips dotted about like stars. There were no tumours. The Professor of Oncology excused himself for a minute or so, to give us time to decide.

'Everybody says it's much more terrible than the cancer itself.'

'That can't be. It's got to be worse than a handful of paracetemols but, you know, desperate remedies.'

'Your way with words has finally deserted you,' she said, tears streaming down her face.

'Listen. I believe in you. Heart and soul I believe in you. We're going to beat this. They haven't begun to realise what a real geezer you are.'

'Geezer?'

'Yes! The tough-as-old-boots Liz. We're going to get through this. I love you.'

'To bits, I suppose.'

She was right: the chemo was almost beyond bearing. We divided our time between the oncology wards and being sick at home. I cooked to order, cleaned and swept, cut the grass, weeded the borders. At night, while she slept, I watched television with the sound turned down. For a few days, sometimes as long as a fortnight, she was better, relative to what she had been. Then came the next appointment.

I would have changed places with her in a flash. Something had happened for which there was no remedy. When she was well enough to come downstairs, we carried on as if we were the same people we had always been. Friends and families came to the house, she poked about the garden and even went out in the car alone to supermarkets and garden centres. While she was gone, I used to think of this as a sign, a hopeful indicator that she would somehow be given back to me. By now she had lost most of her hair and sported a series of piratical head scarves. About these she could even make merry. But, as the days and weeks wore on, her smile became more ghostly. She was not going into remission – but leaving me. I took to sleeping downstairs on the couch.

'What on earth are you doing down here?' she asked incredulously, one early morning.

'I am your household god,' I explained. 'A lar.'

'Shouldn't you be in the hearth?'

'I'm taking the room itself to be the hearth. How do you feel?'

'Lousy. I came down for a camomile.'

'Let me make it.'

'When it comes, it's not coming down the chimney,' she smiled, rocking back against the radiator and hanging onto it as though she had only just discovered that we had such a thing in the house. We both knew what she was talking about.

The day after she finished the last of the chemotherapy, she had a moderate stroke and was admitted to the Radcliffe, on the other side of the London Road. It was, I realised at once, the end. All of her that mattered in the world, the fierce intelligence that had squared up to life and looked it in the eye, had gone. What was left untouched was her memory. God knows how much she exercised it when we were not there, but for many of those who visited it was a sign that all was not lost. By her bedside, paperbacks, crosswords and Sudoku grids piled up as though in a little while she would sit up and take notice. Photographs of her grandchildren were pinned to the wall. There were plans to move her to a hospice, where there was a garden and a view of trees.

I went to see her twice a day, as I had done when she was in the Churchill. Only after her death did the GP tell me that she knew what the stroke masked. She knew that the cancer had established itself in her bones, from which there was no way back. She asked him not to tell me or her children because of the grief it would cause us. She was so silent, so listless in the stroke ward because she had performed this last act of selflessness – and then let go. Her will to live had withered and died and only her memory remained. That, and a fractious heart. The body, the flesh and blood of her, was being eaten alive.

18

Finally . . .

All this while, my beloved Elizabeth, I have written about you in the third person, as if to command the right words and give your story its proper measure. You will not mind if I speak about you now as you are to me still and will always be.

It took me days to work out what it was that was missing from your hospital room. Walking home from a visit, I realised it was a notebook and pen on your counterpane, or fallen onto the floor beside your bed. All that was in the past.

You were only intermittently lucid. With the vanity that comes with every bedside visit to the dying, I assumed you would recognise me. Nor can I live without the belief that you did. Your eyes would search mine patiently, their great beauty undimmed. And then, as if you had risen and left the room completely, they would close. I sat holding your hand, watching you sleep, hardly able to breathe.

In the last days, I loved you for being bad-tempered and peremptory for it was the faint glimmer of who you had been. But to quote from your very first notebook, if

I stood you up sideways you would be marked absent. You died twenty days after your seventy-eighth birthday and when I came out of the hospital that night my legs and arms gave way and I hit the ground like a sack, like a felled beast. Something we tried never to talk about had come along and kicked my own life-support system out of the wall. I lay on the wet grass, utterly helpless.

It happened again crossing the London Road. Peter was with me and dragged me by my heels to a pub, propping me up on the bench of a picnic table. It was dark and the lights of cars swept past. I wanted to stop them all and tell the passengers how wonderful you were. Soon enough, an ambulance passed, on its way with someone else's history. But this was ours.

We walked, Peter and three of your four children, to the pub nearest the house. The night sky seemed to me to fall like soot. We sat in the beer garden, laughing and crying. I found a thought you would have inspected with your usual caution. Nothing is forever. But then again, everything is forever. And there we sat, all of us, while in the houses opposite, bedroom lights went on and the men of the house, as was their duty, bolted the back door to keep the bad things at bay. Or perhaps, to prevent the good things from leaving home.

But then, you know all about this. Don't you?

The Eulogy Delivered at the Funeral of Elizabeth Stewart North (1932–2010) by Dr Peter Thompson, St Cross College, Oxford

Hearing and being heard, the essence of contract bridge; themes in a treasured life. Liz heard us. By which I mean something more than that she was a good listener. She delivered hospitality and understanding to her siblings, children, and friends, remembered birthdays and anniversaries, kept family connections; but above and beyond that she heard in us something of our essence – and her own. In our individual and collective dissonance she heard music – harmonies and rhythms – and tapped her toes to them.

She had a voice and wished it to be heard, not only through her writing. She wished it be heard on the subject of cruise missiles, gender stereotypes and the major conclusions of Western thought. In conversation there were considerations to be weighed in the balance, remarks various to be addressed, points to be got across. She had a distinctive laugh and wished that to be heard in the paper games she taught us to play and in whose successive familial evolutions she took delight. She wished to be heard in the lives of her children and grandchildren and in Brian's life – and she was. And yet there were surely things she wished she'd said but never quite did.

Neither the art of hearing nor of being heard came effortlessly to her. She needed solitude to perfect both. A room of her own, space to think. We were the beneficiaries of that solitude, for hers was a life animated by a generous, wise and proud spirit – a spirit of the kind described by the psalmist: I have been young and am now grown old, yet I have not seen the righteous forsaken, nor their seed beg for bread.

If she occasionally spoke of Ruby Walsh when she meant Ruby Keeler, commended the three Ronnies and sometimes muddled offside and offspin, it doesn't matter now. Hearing and being heard. She can't hear us, but we hear her still.